Read and Write every day

ESOL Literacy Teacher's Book

Dave Butler

Information for teachers

Acknowledgements

Many thanks to several people who have made this book possible. Firstly, thank you to Linda McFall and Kyle Bettley for breathing life into this book and to Susan Leitch, the author's partner teacher for many years, especially for her enthusiasm to discuss materials and teaching techniques, often long after the end of class! Thanks to everyone at Glasgow Clyde College who has supported the author during his time teaching ESOL Literacies, this book couldn't have happened without them. A huge thank you to my dad, Alan Butler, for his expert proofreading. Thanks to the author's very good friend Tom Porter for agreeing to feature in the 'My friend' unit. Last but not least, many thanks to Amina Naveed from design_eyra for beautifully formatting and designing this book. You can find her at aminanaveed794@gmail.com. The images used in this series are from www.depositphotos.com, www.istockphoto.com, www.pixabay.com and www.unsplash.com.

About the author

Dave Butler has over 20 years' experience of teaching ESOL and has been teaching groups of ESOL Literacy learners for 15 years. He holds the CELTA, DELTA and SQA TESOL Literacies qualifications. He's also a teacher trainer on the CELTA and SQA TESOL Literacies courses at Glasgow Clyde College. He enjoys learning Spanish, playing Subbuteo and banter with his family and friends.

Disclaimer

With the exception of myself, Isaac Ellis-Jones, Susan Leitch and Tom Porter, the texts focusing on individuals in this series have been invented for educational purposes. The names and details in these texts are the products of the author's imagination. Any resemblance to actual persons, living or dead, or actual events is purely coincidental.

More materials, classroom ideas and videos

A Student's Book and Workbook accompany this Teacher's Book. The former is packed with reading, writing, numeracy, vocabulary and phonics tasks for ESOL Literacy students while the Workbook contains tasks to set the students for homework, all linked to the work done using the Student's Book. For Power Point slides to use in class, supplementary worksheets, videos for students and teachers and classroom tips and ideas, go to the following site: www.esolbooks.com. Please contact the author to join an email list and receive news of any updates: davebutler@esolbooks.com.

How to use this book

The Teacher's Book outlines how to use the material in the Student's Book and Workbook and suggests extra tasks. For a free Answer key, visit www.esolbooks.com.

Feedback

Please send feedback to the following e-mail address: davebutler@esolbooks.com.

Teacher's Book Contents

Teaching approach	**Page**
Reading and writing	09
Phonics	17
Spelling	20
Numeracy	20
Vocabulary	21
Listening	22
Grammar	23
Revision	23
Homework	23
Technology	24

Suggested lesson plans:

Unit 1	28	Unit 8	66
Unit 2	38	Unit 9	70
Unit 3	43	Unit 10	74
Unit 4	49	Unit 11	78
Unit 5	52	Unit 12	82
Unit 6	58	Unit 13	85
Unit 7	63	Unit 14	89

Extra materials	92
Games and warmers	148
References	190

Student's Book Contents

Unit	Page	Vocabulary	Speaking/reading/writing
1: Me	7	College and the classroom	Describe yourself and your class
2: I like TV	35	Free time activities	Hobbies
3: My day	47	Routines and days of the week	Describe your routine and your favourite day
4: I like the bus	69	Vehicles	Transport and future plans
5: My city	83	Places in a town/city	Describe your town/city, flat and neighbours
6: Food	107	Food	Food and mealtimes
7: The weather	129	The weather Months of the year	Describe the weather in countries you know
8: Happy days	145	Christmas	Special occasions
9: My flat	167	Rooms and furniture	Describe your flat and possessions
10: My country	183	Countries and continents Colours	Describe countries
11: My friend	199		Describe friends and classmates
12: Jobs	209	Jobs	Describe jobs
13: I'm sick	221	Body parts, illnesses, treatment	What you do when you are sick Understanding a text; signs
14: Clothes	235	Clothes Colours (revision)	Describe your clothes and your classmates' clothes

Numeracy	**Phonics**
Numeracy in addresses Numbers 0-10 (numeric form)	s, c, t sh and ch
Numbers 10-20 (numeric form)	ing
Time-telling	ay e and ee
Numbers 0-100 (numeric form)	ing in ‘going to’ (revision)
Numeracy in addresses (revision) Years	c and k
Prices and using money	‘Magic e’, e.g. like
	Short vowel sounds with o, i and u
Dates (numeric and written) and ordinal numbers	Final y (/i:/)
Numbers 1-10 (written form)	s for plural nouns o and oo
Describing populations in millions	ee and oo
	s for third person
	Er; s for third person (revision)
Numeracy in health	ee and ea
Prices and using money Special offers	ing in ‘I’m wearing’ (revision)

Teaching approach

Reading and writing

The texts in the Student's Book aim to be relevant to ESOL literacy groups and graded to their level, meaning that they include high-frequency words and short sentences. The first lines are the simplest for the weaker students who may only read these while the latter sentences are more complex for the stronger learners. The suggested approach in terms of staging is below, divided into 'before', 'while' and 'after' reading stages.

1. **Before reading: oral focus/vocabulary work/prediction tasks**

   Let's use the first text in the Student's Book about 'Mohammad' as an example. Introduce the context by displaying a few pictures of Mohammad and his interests:

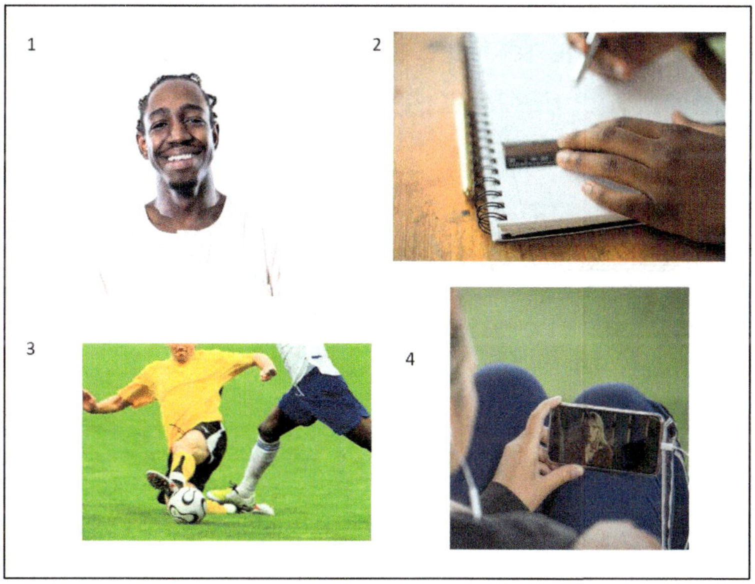

   Introduce Mohammad and put the learners into pairs/small groups with the task, "What can you see?" Elicit more about him, e.g. "How old is he? Is he a teacher or a student? What does he like?" to help the students predict the text, making the reading tasks more achievable. We want the group to know the contents before they get stuck into the text so that they can concentrate primarily on reading without trying to interpret this for meaning too.

This also takes advantage of our learners' 'spiky profile.' While many students at other ESOL levels tend to be more uniform across the four skills, students in basic ESOL Literacy groups tend to have a stronger level of speaking and listening compared to their literacy level. We can exploit this by including speaking tasks based on the topic of the day before any reading and writing work.

2. While reading

a. Reading aloud

In contrast to stronger classes where students often read silently, reading aloud is essential at this level. Doing so allows the students to link sounds and spelling while the teacher gauges the learners' progress. See below for a way to approach this, based on a series of DVDs originally produced by the London Literacy Unit and Spiegel and Sunderland's 'Teaching Basic Literacy to ESOL Learners.'

i. The teacher displays the text on, ideally, an interactive whiteboard. If this isn't available, a projector connected to a laptop is fine.
ii. The teacher reads the text aloud, running their finger under the words as they go and maintaining eye contact with the students. Ask a few comprehension questions, for instance, for the text about Mohammad in unit 1, ask, "What's his name? Where is he from?"
iii. There are a few variations for the next step. You could have the whole class read aloud with you ('choral reading'). Alternatively, you could read each line aloud and then the whole class repeats this as one ('echo reading'), line-by-line.
iv. Focus on phonics by pointing at key words in the text and asking, "What's that?" A key strategy for students is to use the sound we often produce for the first letter in a word (the 'initial consonant' sound). Exploit the text to help the group develop this skill, e.g. for the word 'my', point at the 'm' and ask "What's this sound?" You're highlighting sounds here, eliciting /m/ (like the sound we make for delicious food!) rather than the /em/ we would say for the letter 'm.'
v. Pair students to read aloud together ('paired reading'). They can either take turns to read the whole text or read sentence-by-sentence. Modelling this task through two students reading aloud as an example of what you want them to do makes

the task clear before they have a go. It makes sense to pair weaker students together for this so that you can help them while they are on task. If anyone is struggling with a word, point at the first letter and ask them, "What's the sound?" but don't persevere for too long with this, just tell them the word if necessary, they'll get another chance to read it. Stronger students can read the text more than once while weaker learners might just read the first line or two.

vi. After a few minutes of paired reading, go back to the board and nominate students to read a sentence. If you're confident that a weaker learner can manage the first line, as you've seen them do it while monitoring, then this is a great chance to boost their confidence. Nominate stronger students for the sentences towards the end of texts.

I vividly remember the first time I asked students to read a text aloud. My fears were this: will the learners refuse to read aloud, perhaps viewing this as childish or too easy? Will they protest that it's ridiculous to repeat a task like this so many times? However, my experience is the opposite: students love reading aloud and are very happy to do so multiple times. If a learner does start complaining, it's usually a sign that they've reached a point where their reading level is too good for an ESOL literacy class. If you agree, then this may be cause to celebrate though remember that they also need a good enough writing level to be moved up a level to a beginners' class.

b. Reading Comprehension

The Student's Book includes several reading tasks for each text to incorporate more reading practice after the students have read aloud. The first exercises are designed to be the easiest for the weaker learners, e.g. matching sentence halves or gap-fills, while the latter tasks are more difficult comprehension tasks, e.g. true or false questions, short-answer questions or ordering tasks.

Weaker students might only manage a proportion of these tasks while stronger learners can proceed at a faster pace. Don't feel that everyone has to answer every question of every task. While monitoring, grade your feedback according to a learner's level, for example, for stronger students attempting true/false questions you can say, "Well done, four answers are good but change two", highlighting which ones include incorrect responses. For instance, perhaps they got questions one and two correct so you can highlight three to six and say "change two answers." An extension task like this will keep them busy while you help the weaker learners. If they answer all of the questions correctly then you can ask them to look at the false responses and change them so that they are true. Model this task by doing the first one with them. For example, for the true/false question, 'Mohammad is from Glasgow', cross out 'Glasgow', elicit the answer and write 'Sudan' above it.

3. After reading

a. Focus on Dolch/Fry List words

The Dolch and Fry Lists feature the most common words in English. You can guess which words will be in this list (for instance, be, do, have) or search online to see all of them. The aim of the Student's Book and Workbook is to give the group regular exposure to these words through reading texts aloud, various exercises in each book and through writing tasks. Initially, students can use 'sounding out' strategies to read these words, in which we string together the sounds of individual letters. Through repetition of target activities they will hopefully reach 'whole word recognition', where they see a word and can read it without sounding out individual letters. This is my usual process to help the students practise these high-frequency words:

- After the students have read aloud and done some comprehension tasks, display the text on the board but with some high-frequency words numbered. Ask the students, "Which number is 'like'? 'From'?" and elicit the initial sound. Do this as a group and if the students seem comfortable, nominate individuals.

Mohammad

1 2 3 4 5
My name is Mohammad. I am from
6 7 8 9
Sudan. I am 28 years old. I live in
10
Glasgow. I like Glasgow. I am a
11
student. I like football and You Tube. I
play football with my friends.

- Include regular practice through 'LSCWC.' This refers to the 'look-say-cover-write-check' technique whereby students look at a word, read it aloud (saying the word to link the sound and spelling), cover the word with their hand, write it and finally, check it's correct. You can write words on the board for students to do this in their notebooks or prepare a worksheet. The Student's Book and Workbook include LSCWC tasks in each unit. Use the cards to run a LSCWC slot in class and back this up with the same task for homework. Covering the words is essential as students need to push themselves to spell words without copying if they are to reach a level of independent writing. However, reassure them that if they have any problem then it's fine to lift their hands to have another look.

- Each text in the Student's Book is followed by a gap-fill exercise after the comprehension tasks in which most of the gapped words are from the Dolch/Fry List, for example, see page 9 in unit 1. Help the students with this while monitoring by saying the word they are looking for. If necessary, they can copy from the original complete text but encourage them to try to do this without copying. For the second attempt, the aim is for the group to improve their spelling of these words through LSCWC, i.e. each learner covers the first paragraph and then fills in the gaps. Fast finishers can repeat the LSCWC process one more time by looking at the text to memorise a few words at a time, covering it and then writing these words into their notebooks rather than the Student's Book. Remember that it's fine if the weaker learners don't finish the whole page.

- Prepare three sets of word cards by folding and cutting a blank A4 sheet into 8 rectangular pieces. Assign each student a number and have them copy a Dolch/Fry List word onto separate cards, for example, Samira copies the word 'like' onto three separate pieces of paper.

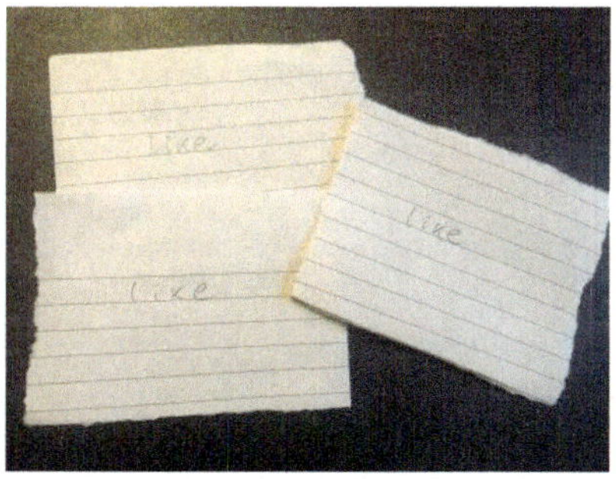

It's important to enlist the students throughout all this as they then take ownership of the process. Divide the cards up into three groups of 11 cards and divide the students up into three groups by level so that you can give more help to the weaker learners while they are on task. After handing each group a set of cards, there are various tasks that you can now set the students, as described below.

- After the learners lay the cards out in front of them, the teacher says a word and the first student to pick up the card and show it to you wins a point for their team.
- The learners work together to look at a card and read it aloud.
- The students take a card and go through the 'LSCWC' steps to practise.
- One student takes a card and reads it aloud but doesn't show it to the others in their group. After attempting to write it, they are shown the card so they can check their spelling. Grade the task here, for instance, weaker learners can just attempt the first letter or allow them to ask, "Show me please?" and be granted a quick look at the word. However, they shouldn't simply copy the word. They have a quick look, turn the card over and write the word.

As with other tasks, help the weakest group more while keeping an eye on the stronger learners. As this is a great way to regularly revise words that the students learn, don't throw these cards away after class! Instead, add to the three piles regularly by making new cards after reading future texts. Note that the use of these cards can be done on the first day you read a text together or the next class after the students read the same text again as revision.

- The Workbook contains a variety of tasks to give further practice of Dolch/Fry List words which are in the texts in the Student's Book. These include exercises such as word-matching, word searches and LSCWC. See below for some extracts.

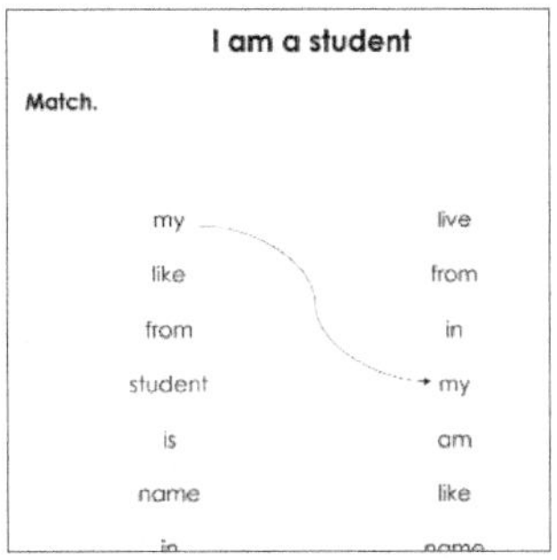

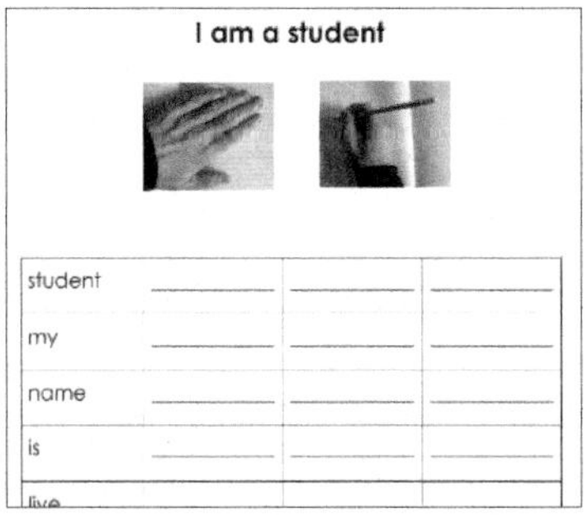

b. Writing

As a general rule of thumb, students should discuss a topic before they write about it in a subsequent stage. For instance, in unit 1, speaking about themselves before they write this as a text will help the students to link sounds and spelling, writing down words and phrases that they've used themselves orally.

While higher level ESOL groups can cope with free writing tasks, at this level we need to give more support. Spelling practice through LCSWC work before the students write their texts will help them build up towards freer writing. This is incorporated into the material in the Student's Book, often to help prepare learners for writing tasks. For example, the LSCWC task below precedes a task where the students write about themselves in unit 1.

name	___________	___________	___________
from	___________	___________	___________
live	___________	___________	___________
years old	___________	___________	___________
student	___________	___________	___________
like	___________	___________	___________

Following this preparation, choose a student to model the writing task. Involve the class to generate a text about one of the learners, which you write on the board. Tell the students that this is the text they will now write but about themselves. Remove this model as we want to push the students to write without copying. However, allow them to "have a quick look" at the model text in the coursebook (e.g. for unit 1, the text about Mohammad on page 8), if necessary. Make it clear that it's fine to look at the model text again and again but that it's preferable to try to memorise spellings and use phonics to aid their writing rather than copy. Help in monitoring, especially by encouraging the students to sound out words in order to spell them.

There's plenty of scope for more writing practice here:

i. Monitor and encourage the students to correct errors such as spelling, letter formation, writing on the line and spacing. If they can improve their text, that's enough, i.e. let some errors go - don't be a perfectionist. As the group will be self-correcting, they must use pencils so take plenty of stationery into class! Give the weaker students more help while keeping an eye on the stronger learners and keeping them busy. There are two main ways to do this: firstly, highlight a few errors for them to self-correct. Secondly, encourage them to add to their texts. For instance, after writing about themselves, if a fast finisher has only written one sentence about their hobbies, ask them to write more about this. When everyone has written at least a few lines, have them read their texts aloud in pairs.

ii. The students write their texts again but they use the LSCWC approach sentence-by-sentence rather than simply copying. Clarify that if they have any problem, they can have a quick look again but they must cover when they write, not copy. Set this task for homework also.

When it comes to letter formation, I find a wide range of ability in my classes. While some students form letters perfectly in terms of both size and form, others really struggle. It's quick and easy to create your own handwriting worksheets by using a website such as 'All Kids Network.' You could input a text from class, for instance, into the worksheet creator, for it to magically produce printable worksheets featuring tasks such as the one below, where the students trace over the dots. The Workbook includes examples like the one below for most of the texts the students read in class.

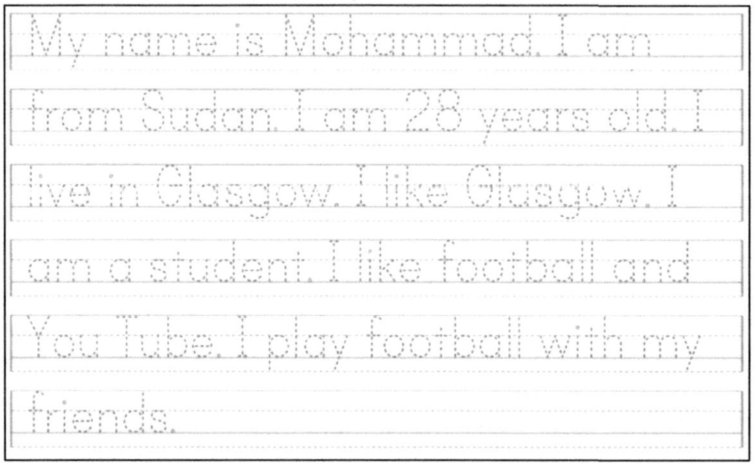

Phonics

If students use phonics effectively, it is a great way to improve their literacy level by using the common sounds of each letter when reading or writing. At an early level, they can use this skill to 'sound out' words. Reading aloud as a class offers the teacher the opportunity to encourage the group to notice sound-spelling combinations within a context. This is clearly illustrated in the LLU+ DVDs previously referred to, in which after reading the text aloud a few times, the teacher points at a word, asking, "What's this word?" and then points at the first letter, asking "What's the sound for this letter?" Regularly doing this for about ten words in each text will help the students build up an awareness of the sounds commonly linked to letters.

In addition to this regular exploitation of words within texts, it's effective to plan a slot in which the group practises just one or two letter-sound combinations. For example, the two sounds 'sh' and 'ch' are focused on in unit 1. Using pictures which represent words including the sounds sets the context in which to zoom in on the phonics work. Concentrating on two sounds rather than just one enables the teacher to incorporate more concrete tasks for the students. For example, if we focused just on 'sh' then a gap-fill would be pointless but if we study 'ch' as well as 'sh', then asking them to fill in the gaps with sh or ch is much more interesting and enables the teacher to gauge the students' progress. Plan some speaking before the students get stuck into the reading and writing tasks. Let's look in more detail at the exact staging for one of these phonics sessions, using the sh/ch work in unit 1 as an example.

a) Show the pictures from page 31 on the whiteboard. Pair the students up with the task, "What can you see?" Drill the words in open-class feedback.

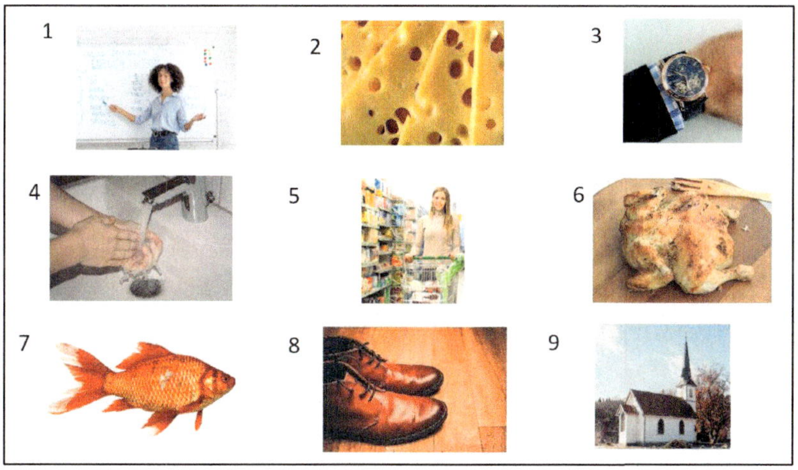

b) Focus on "English teacher" and drill the phrase. Clarify the spelling, board the phrase and then elicit the sounds for these digraphs. Ask the students if they know any more words with the sh sound. Repeat for the ch sound, drilling some of this vocabulary.
c) Continue the oral work by testing if the students can distinguish between the two sounds. Dictate the words which were used earlier for the students to respond by saying 'c' 'h' or 's' 'h' (in this case they say the letters rather than sounds). Alternatively, the learners write sh or ch on separate pieces of paper/a mini whiteboard to hold up. For instance, the teacher says "chicken" and the students respond appropriately.
d) Introduce the written form with tasks that go from easy to difficult, from receptive to productive (refer to pages 31-33 of the Student's Book for these tasks). Power Point slides on www.esolbooks.com include the images above as well as words for the group to read aloud.
e) Plan tasks to revise this, for example:
    - Flash cards.
    - Work with the group to create a mind map (see below). Write this on the board, including any words the students know, especially any names of their classmates (e.g. Shahnaz) or countries they are from (e.g. China). Repeat the process for ch before putting the students into groups with large sheets of paper and markers to create a poster for the classroom wall.

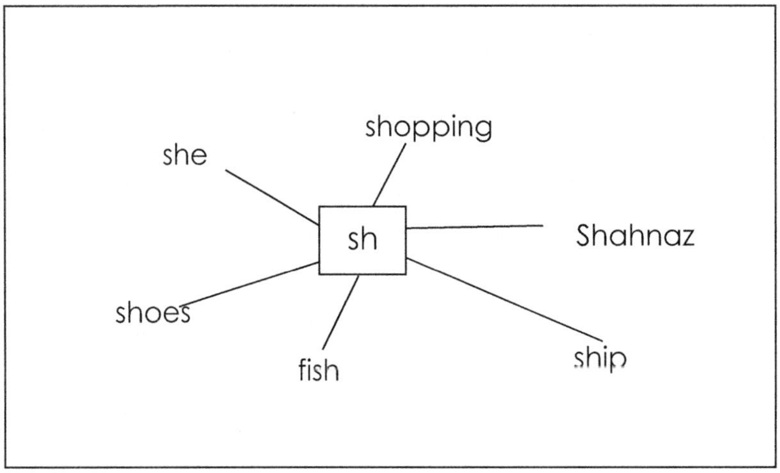

f) The end of each unit in the Student's Book includes some practice of initial consonants. For instance, here's the task at the end of unit 1:

a b c

Listen and circle.

1.	f	m	s
2.	c	t	d
3.	r	h	w
4.	b	m	c
5.	s	t	b

For each line, the teacher says a word and the students circle the first letter in that word. For example, for line 1, the teacher says "my" and the learners circle the letter 'm' – stronger students can go beyond this to write the full word if they can. Use vocabulary the students know, such as their names, countries or any words learnt during the week. Throw in a few words that they will know but which haven't featured during the week to encourage them to really listen for the sound.

Here's a suggested list for the task above:

1. my
2. teacher
3. we
4. college
5. banana
6. chicken
7. read
8. swimming
9. she
10. not

g) Finally, the vocabulary lessons in the Student's Book incorporate some phonics work. To be precise, each lexical set includes practice of initial consonants in which the students can use the sound-spelling combination to write the first letter of the words.

Should we start by teaching the alphabet and the sounds of each letter in the first few classes? I prefer a 'top-down approach' to exploit texts to focus on areas such as initial consonant sounds. This takes advantage of vocabulary the students already know and have seen in a context to zoom in on letter-sound combinations. You can find an excellent summary of this debate in Spiegel and Sunderland's 'Teaching Basic Literacy to ESOL Learners.'

Sending a video to your students which clarifies the letter-sound combinations for each letter of the alphabet, using pictures to back this up with context, gives them an excellent self-study tool. Go to www.esolbooks.com for a video you can download and send.

Spelling

The main tools to help students with spelling include:

1. Encouraging learners to use phonics to sound out words which they are trying to spell. Awareness of more advanced phonics such as digraphs, rimes (longer 'chunks' within words, for example, ing, ed, er), sounding out beyond the initial consonant, awareness of silent letters and learning vowel sounds will help them to improve.
2. Repetition of Dolch/Fry List words in various contexts in reading and writing tasks is key. It's only through reading and writing a word again and again that students can know words well enough to spell them. LSCWC and the use of flash cards offer an excellent way to ensure repeat exposure to these words. Furthermore, the tasks in the Student's Book and Workbook include plenty of repetition.

Numeracy

The Student's Book includes some basic numeracy work such as numbers in numeric and written form, dates, time-telling and prices. This is kept very simple and focused on within a context. Resources such as Skills for Life and SQAs ESOL Literacy pack include more examples of numeracy taught within a practical context. Go to the references section at the back of this book for details of these.

Vocabulary

The Student's Book uses pictures to help groups learn new vocabulary as a lexical set. Not only are these a clear and easy way to clarify meaning but they also help us to ensure a student-centred approach as you can put the learners into pairs with the simple instruction, "What can you see?" As discussed, oral work precedes the written form. Using the lexical set of classroom objects in unit 1 as an example, here's the suggested plan for staging this particular vocabulary work:

a) Introduce the topic through a couple of simple questions, e.g. "Do you have a pencil? Do you have a notebook?"
b) Display pictures of the objects on the whiteboard (see below; you can access Power Point slides like this on www.esolbooks.com) or, if you have time, prepare cut-out cards for the students to spread out on their desks.

Look at the Extra Materials section at the back of this book for a range of cards to use for each unit in the Student's Book. Whether you display pictures on the board or use flash cards, the students work together to name the items.

c) Clarify the words and help the students with pronunciation in open-class feedback. Following this, nominate individuals to check how well they have retained the vocabulary (e.g. "Hana, number 3?"). The students test each other in pairs in the same way to consolidate.
d) Drill short phrases to give more context for the words, e.g. "I have a pencil", "I don't have a rubber." The question "Do you have a rubber?" will be well-used during the year! This works well as a 'substitution drill', e.g. Teacher: "Hana, rubber", Hana: "I don't have a rubber."

e) Now the students know the oral form of the word, they are ready for the letter gap-fill on pages 19-20, which further exploits the language for some work on initial consonants. Say the words for the students while monitoring if necessary. It's fine if the weaker learners only do the first of these two pages while the stronger students attempt the more difficult page which follows. The learners should use phonics for this but reassure them that if they have any problem with the second of these pages then they can have a quick look at the first page again. An alternative to displaying the words on the board is to prepare cut-out cards and give them to the learners. There are cards for this in the 'Extra Materials' section at the back of the book. See pages 93-94 for instructions and flash cards for the lexical set of classroom objects mentioned above, which could be used in this way:

   i. Give the students the picture cards first without the words. They work in pairs to name the words. Clarify the vocabulary and help the class with pronunciation. You could consolidate this through the students testing each other in pairs, i.e. a student takes a card and asks their partner, "What's that?"
   ii. The students work in pairs to match the pictures to the words. Monitor to help, encouraging the learners to use the initial consonant and check each group has done this correctly.
   iii. Use the board to show the words and elicit the initial consonant sounds, silent letters, any interesting phonics, e.g. digraphs like sh/ch, rimes such as 'ing' or 'er.'
   iv. The students remove the pictures so that they only have the words in front of them. Say the words (e.g. Teacher: "notebook!") and the first student to hold up the word is awarded a point for their team. Finally, the students read the words on the cards aloud.
   v. The students move onto the letter gap-fill tasks in the Student's Book. In unit 1, for instance, they turn to pages 19-20.

Listening

Some of the units in the Student's Book include listening tasks. For some, you can find an audio file on www.esolbooks.com. Others include the teacher as text. As writing anything beyond a word or two while listening is too demanding for learners at this level, students can write very short answers instead. For example, on page 56 of the Student's Book, the learners listen to the teacher say the time and write it in number format. Another option is to give the students two or three very simple questions orally to which they respond, also orally, with very short answers. For instance, for the listening task on page 244, where the group listens to a dialogue between a customer and shop assistant in a clothes shop, the questions, "What does he buy? How much is it? How does he pay?" would be manageable. Alternatively, there are questions on that page with a minimal amount of text.

We can often exploit audio to highlight useful language within the text. For example, with the clothes shop listening, play the audio again and stop it just after key language such as "Can you help me please?" to ask, "What did he say?" After eliciting and drilling a few phrases this sets you up for a customer-shop assistant role play.

Grammar

I don't teach so much grammar at this level. Any grammar in the Student's Book has been selected as it is appropriate to this level and also enables work on phonics. For example, the use of a gerund to follow 'like' (e.g. I like shopping) allows work on the extremely common 'ing' rime/phonogram. In terms of clarification for the students, keep it simple, for instance, "we use 'ing' after we say 'I like'" would be sufficient.

Revision

Repetition is key in language learning so factor in revision tasks throughout. For example, the day after the reading and writing class about 'Mohammad', practise this again the next day through more paired reading of the same text. The Dolch List flash cards are also an excellent way to repeat and revise. In addition to the recycling of language through the Student's Book tasks, set homework from the Workbook every day at the end of each class to encourage more revision.

Homework

I recently spoke to an ex-student of mine who started in a basic ESOL Literacy group but has since been moved up to a pre-intermediate class. For a student who couldn't read at all on day one but has reached a good literacy level for a pre-intermediate learner, he's a real success story! When I asked him how he managed this, he explained that, in addition to homework tasks set by the teacher, he reads texts from the day's lessons again and again and copies them out several times, he watches ESOL lessons on You Tube and borrows books from the library. He does have lots of spare time which some of his peers don't have, for example, those with jobs and/or a busy family life. However, he told me that he studies after class for hours and the point is clear: studying in college is great but if you really want to read and write well you need to back this up with lots of self-study at home.

The aim of the Student's Workbook is to provide an easy way for teachers to set homework for their class. However, have regular chats with your students about the need to go beyond this. LSCWC on any text they write in class and re-reading the texts from their lessons are good ways to do more. In addition, take your group to the library (if your institution has one) to borrow graded readers and show them how to find You Tube teachers (tech-savvy students know some good ones, often from their home country, who use varying degrees of their own language to teach some basic English). They can watch and re-watch videos you post to a class What's App group (see the suggestions under 'Technology' later in this chapter for details). Obviously, we need to be aware of the limitations that restrict students with busy lives but make it clear that putting in the hours really is the only way to make significant progress. Use a case study of one of your ex-students like the one I described above to explain how to succeed. In addition, find out your learners' goals and remind them of this to keep them motivated.

Get into the habit of setting homework at the end of each class and checking it at the beginning. Keep this snappy: set the students up to check in pairs while monitoring to give individual feedback. The tasks are designed to be useful but simple enough to do alone at home.

Technology

If you have a PC room in your institution, then regular visits are a great way to build students' IT skills while giving more reading and writing practice in a different setting. As regards IT skills, there tends to be a wide range in most classes. Some students have never used a computer while others are adept at surfing the web. In terms of language work, there are some websites with suitable online tasks, such as Excellence Gateway, NATECLAs online graded readers, ESOL Courses and Many Things (go to www.esolbooks.com for a page of useful links such as these). However, there aren't so many websites which are appropriate for this level so I often prepare my own tasks. For instance, exploit a word processing programme like Microsoft Word to have the group type out any texts they've recently written in class. Teach them how to print their document and highlight a few errors to self-correct, such as punctuation, spelling or adding spaces between words. If your college has a VLE then writing your own quizzes based on the material is an excellent way to revise the work done in class. If you don't, then Microsoft/Google Forms can be used to achieve the same aim.

As many students nowadays have smartphones, a class What's App group is a great way to communicate with them, especially through videos. For example, at the end of a lesson, you can give a learner your phone to record a video of you reading the text of the day aloud for them to practise at home. If you don't want the students to know your mobile number then you can use 'What's App for Business' and use your work phone number. A What's App group is also an excellent way to share a video in which you set homework tasks. Go to www.esolbooks.com to access free downloadable videos of the texts in the Student's Book being read aloud.

Kahoot.com offers a fun and interactive platform for online quizzes with the group. They can work in pairs and use their mobiles to answer questions displayed on the whiteboard. As it takes quite a while to get the learners set up for this, I prepare one big quiz at the end of each unit but you could give the class smaller quizzes after work on specific areas, for instance after phonics lessons. You can create your own quizzes for free but with access to only a limited number of question types. To access a wider range of question types you will need to pay a subscription.

Search 'TeacherGCC' (case specific) on Kahoot to find quizzes which are linked to the Student's Book. I pay for the Pro Plan (around £35 per year) so you may have to sign up to the same package to use the questions. Alternatively, you can save a copy and edit the questions.

Suggested Lesson Plans

Unit 1: Me

Speaking/reading/writing: providing personal information; punctuation – introduction to using capital letters and full stops; describing your class

Vocabulary: classroom objects

Phonics: initial consonants - s, c, t; digraphs – sh and ch; initial consonants – end-of-unit revision

Numeracy: numbers 0-10 in numeric form; contextualised numbers in an address (telephone number, flat position, postcode).

Extra Material: Vocabulary flash cards; numbers 0-10 flash cards; numbers 0-10 bingo

Teaching your first class with a new group

I don't use any materials for the first class. I know, I've spent ages writing the Student's Book which you've just bought and now I'm saying not to use it. Well, don't use it just yet! My main aims for the first class are this:

1. Do any necessary administration such as registration, getting student cards, filling in bursary/bus pass forms etc.
2. Set speaking tasks to enable the teacher and students to get to know each other.
3. Set some very basic reading and writing tasks as a diagnostic exercise.
4. Establish class rules.

1. Administration

I try not to cover too much on the first day in order to leave time for registration and any other issues that arise. As many students like to resolve matters such as bus passes or applying for childcare as soon as possible, prioritise this and everyone will get off to a calm start to the new year.

2. **Get to know the students**

After modelling the language by introducing yourself, drill some phrases such as, "My name is ....", "I am from....", "I live in Glasgow", "I like...", "Nice to meet you" - "Nice to meet you too." Put the students into small groups to introduce each other. Ask a few individuals to introduce themselves in open-class feedback before repeating the task as a mingle.

Note that this opening stage is purely oral, thus playing to the students' strengths, allowing them to get to know each other without the strain of any reading/writing tasks.

3. **Reading and writing diagnostic**

a. See if the students can remember personal information about you by asking questions such as, "Where am I from?" and "What's my job?" Board this as a brief text, for example, "My name is Dave. I am from England. I live in Glasgow. I am a teacher. I like football and TV."
b. After hearing the teacher read the text aloud, the teacher and students read aloud as a group. Monitor while the students copy the text but mostly as a diagnostic tool to gauge the general writing level.
c. Pair the students up to read the text aloud, monitoring while they do so. Help them while they are on task but hang back as much as possible as this too is a diagnostic tool, this time to gauge their reading level.
d. Use a student as a model for the subsequent writing task. Include the students by asking questions such as, "What is her name? Where is she from?" in order to build a text which you board and read aloud, e.g. "My name is Asma. I am from Sudan. I live in Glasgow. I am a student. I like college and the gym." Remove the text and see if anyone can write without copying as a diagnostic tool. Allow anyone who is struggling to look at the earlier text about the teacher as a crib sheet. Again, monitor but mostly with a diagnostic aim, noting any common issues. For example, if many have problems with letter formation or writing on the line then this is an area you could work on in a future class. For instance, you could prepare a worksheet to integrate remedial work on this during the first

week of classes. Finally, the students read their texts aloud in pairs before employing the LSCWC method, sentence-by-sentence, to rewrite their texts.

4. Establish class rules

It's also important to go through the rules for the class. Elicit these from the students, by asking questions such as, "What time do we start class?" On the first day, I keep this quite snappy but it is important to make the rules clear, whatever they are in your institution. For example, if good attendance is essential then students need to know that they will lose their place/travel bursary if they don't attend.

This could be worth reinforcing in a future class through the Language Experience Approach (LEA), which takes advantage of a common experience/shared context to work on reading and writing. In the context of class rules, you could follow these steps:

a) Show some pictures that represent the rules, for instance, a picture of a clock to show that students must come on time. Put the students into pairs/small groups to tell each other what they can see. Although there is no material for this in the Student's Book, there are Power Point slides on www.esolbooks.com.
b) Elicit the rules and board this as a text, for example:

> College Rules
>
> 1. Come on time.
> 2. Come every day.
> 3. Speak English.
> 4. No food in class.
> 5. No phones.

c) Read the text aloud as a group and, after the learners have copied the text, they read aloud once again in pairs ('paired reading').
d) The students practise writing through LSCWC.
e) Record a video and post it to the class What's App group.

A quick note on speaking English versus the students' first language (L1) in class. When I started teaching ESOL, I was told that we mustn't allow any L1 in the classroom. Whilst I do believe that students speaking as much English as possible is beneficial to the whole group, I'm not quite as insistent on this as I am with other levels. A little L1 when students are really struggling can help clarify meaning which is vital before learners attempt reading and writing tasks. Try to limit this but a little is fine for me. If there are students speaking a lot of L1 in my class I ask myself, "Are my instructions not clear? Is my teacher talk (TT) graded?" as often this happens as a result of problems with TT/classroom management.

I usually find that the above is enough for the first class but if I have time I try to set up a What's App group too.

We can start using the material for our second lesson with the group!

1. Mohammad, pages 8-10
   Aims: speaking, reading and writing

   a) See the earlier guidance in the 'Teaching Approach' section on reading aloud and reading comprehension (pages 9-12) which includes detailed instructions for those stages in this lesson.
   b) Get the students mingling to tell each other about themselves. This is a repeat of a speaking task in the previous day's class but you could vary this by having everyone include one piece of false information. Model the task to make it clear for the group, e.g. "My name is Dave, I am 48 years old, I am from Sudan." Students find this quite enjoyable and it makes the repetition more interesting.
   c) The writing frame and LSCWC tasks on page 10 help prepare the students to write about themselves. As on the first day, use yourself or a student to model the personalised writing task, which can be further exploited through LSCWC.

2. Aa Bb Cc, pages 11-15

   Aim: pronunciation – letters of the alphabet; writing - letter formation; punctuation: capitals and lower case

   a) Practise the alphabet orally first. Can the students recite all 26 letters in order? Test them out in pairs and then drill the letters in chunks of three in open-class feedback.
   b) Pages 11–15 offer the chance for various practice tasks. Some of these could be omitted and/or given as homework. Pages 11-13 are receptive and as such, easier. The latter of these involves the teacher saying a letter and the learners circling one of the three choices accordingly. Pronounce these as letters, not sounds, for example, teacher: "letter 's' /es/." Pages 14 and 15 require productive skills from the learners.

3. Mohammad, pages 16-18

   Aim: punctuation – capital letters to begin sentences, for names and countries, using full stops

   a) The material moves from receptive to productive, initially with the students identifying the capital letters and full stops. In feedback, elicit the reasons for these, e.g. capital letters to start sentences, for first names etc.
   b) The subsequent tasks are increasingly productive, culminating in the group copying the complete unpunctuated text while adding capital letters and full stops.
   c) A personalised task follows (page 16) where the students use a key word to write a sentence about themselves. If anyone is struggling, they can refer to the sentences in the original Mohammad text for help. Help the students with punctuation in monitoring – are they using capital letters and full stops? Back up this punctuation work in the subsequent text about 'My class.' For instance, highlight the name 'Asma' and ask, "Do we use a big or small 'a'?", "Why?"

4. College, pages 19-20
   Aims: vocabulary – classroom objects; phonics - initial consonant sounds

   See the earlier guidance in the 'Teaching Approach' section on teaching vocabulary and to see detailed instructions for this lesson (pages 21-22). There are flash cards for this vocabulary in the Extra Materials section at the back of this book.

5. My class, pages 21-23
   Aims: speaking, reading and writing

   a) As a lead in, show some pictures representing 'Asma' and elicit/tell the students about her.
   b) A reading aloud stage and comprehension tasks follow on pages 21-22.
   c) Personalise the lesson by asking questions such as "How many students are in your class? How many teachers do you have?" Drill a few phrases before putting the learners into pairs to speak about their class.
   d) Page 23 helps prepare the class for the subsequent writing task through LSCWC of key words they will use when they describe their class. Elicit a model text for the students and board it, e.g. 'My name is Samira. I go to college 3 days a week. College is Monday, Tuesday and Thursday. We have 10 students in my class. The students are from Iraq, Afghanistan and Sudan. We have one teacher. I like my class.' Remove this while the students write but let them "have a quick look" at the text on page 21 if they need some support. After they finish, they read their texts aloud and then use LSCWC on their texts for more practice. I find that most students can memorise a few words at a time and then cover and write but let the students decide what is manageable.

6. My address, page 24
   Aim: writing your address

   a) Start with some oral practice by asking questions such as "Where do you live? What's your address?" Pair the students up to repeat the task by asking each other the same questions.

b) Display page 24 on the board and read it aloud. Ask some comprehension questions ("What's his postcode?") and model the matching task.
c) Many students know their address orally but carry a record of this (e.g. a scan on their phones) which they copy instead of memorising it. Emphasise the importance of being able to write this from memory but allow them to copy out their address initially on page 24.
d) The students use LSCWC for the subsequent times they write their address. Set more LSCWC for homework and practise this the following day in class. This is also revised in a future unit of the Student's Book.

7. s/c/t, pages 25-26
   Aim: phonics - focus on 3 initial consonant sounds

   a) Show the pictures from page 26 on the whiteboard and then pair the students up to name them. In open-class feedback, nominate different learners for each image and help with pronunciation by drilling as a group.
   b) Board the words 'student', 'teacher' and 'college' and elicit the initial consonant sounds by pointing and asking, "What's the sound for this letter?" Remind the class that there are letters and sounds (letter /es/, sound /s/) and that to read and write we need to learn the sounds for each letter. Clarify the letter and sound for s, c and t before the learners fill in the gaps at the top of page 25.
   c) Continue some oral work by saying the nine words from the first task, one at a time. Students respond by telling you the first letter, e.g. "Teacher: ten", "students: /ti:/" Add other words that learners know at this level, e.g. see, to, come, some, car and include relevant names/countries from the group, if possible, e.g. Syria, Sudan, Samira etc. Do this for a while as a group with students shouting out and then repeat the task, nominating individuals.
   d) If you think the learners can manage it, display words from these earlier tasks on the board for them to read aloud. Firstly, show the words for anyone to shout out. Then nominate individuals, choosing weaker students for easier words.
   e) Consolidate with a reading/writing focus through the table on page 25 and the letter gap-fill on the following page.
   f) Create flash cards and/or a mind map the following day as revision.

8. 1, 2, 3, pages 27-30

   Aim: numeracy: numbers 0-10 in oral and numeric form, including number formation

   a) Hold up some pencils to elicit 'three pencils.' Put the students into pairs to recite numbers 0-10 orally.
   a) Drill the numbers. If the students are good at this, you could push them by introduce some more complex language, e.g. "Which number is after 2? Before 8? Between 4 and 6?"
   b) Try a mingle where the students look around the class and point at various objects, e.g. "Look, two rubbers", "four cups", "ten chairs" etc.
   c) Pages 27-30 give practice of the numbers in numeric form. Practice of the numbers in written form is focused on later in the coursebook. For the 'listen and circle' task, put the words into a context, e.g.
      a. I get up at 6 o'clock.
      b. My friend has 3 children.
      c. My friend's son is 8 years old.
      d. I have 3 bedrooms in my flat.
      e. My friend's daughter is 9 years old.
   d) If the text on page 29 is too difficult for your class, then the students can close their books and turn this into a listening task by you reading out the sentences for them to write the answers as numbers. They check in pairs and then try to remember what these refer to while checking with their partners.
   e) For the final practice task on page 30, put the numbers into a short phrase, e.g.
      a. I usually have 3 cups of coffee.
      b. Break is at 2 o'clock.
      c. We finish class at 4 o'clock.
      d. My friend has 4 children.
      e. His son is 10 years old.
      f. His youngest daughter is 3 years old.
      g. We go to college 4 days a week.
      h. 5 million people live in Scotland.
      i. I go to bed at 10 o'clock.
      j. I got a new t-shirt yesterday. It cost £9.

There is an activity in the Extra Materials section which can be used to revise these numbers. Cut-out cards for numbers 0-10 (pages 96-97) can be given to the learners to put in order. They then mix them up and the teacher can call out numbers for the students to hold up the card. This might be a nice revision task for the following day's class. Bingo, also available in the Extra Materials section, is always a lot of fun for students.

9. sh/ch, pages 31-33
   Aim: phonics – digraphs

   See the 'Teaching approach' section earlier in this book (pages 17-20) for notes on how to help students during phonics tasks. It uses this lesson as an example.

10. abc, page 34
    Aim: phonics - initial consonant sounds

    This page facilitates some phonics work to end the unit. See the earlier guidance in this book in the 'Teaching Approach' section on teaching phonics (pages 17-20) for detailed instructions for this lesson.

    Suggested words below:

1. my
2. teacher
3. we
4. college
5. banana
6. chicken
7. read
8. swimming
9. she
10. not

11. Kahoot Quiz

Aim: revision

Finish the unit with a Kahoot quiz. Search 'TeacherGCC' (case specific) on Kahoot to find the quiz for unit 1.

For a free Answer Key for every unit, visit www.esolbooks.com.

Unit 2: I like TV

Speaking/reading/writing: free time

Vocabulary: lexical set of hobbies

Phonics: 'ing' words

Numeracy: numbers 10-20 in numeric form; review of numbers in context covered in units 1-2

Extra Material: Free time vocabulary flash cards; numbers 10-20 flash cards; numbers 10-20 bingo

1. I like TV, pages 36-37
   Aims: vocabulary - lexical set of hobbies and interests; phonics - initial consonants

   a) For your lead in, elicit some of your hobbies by miming them, e.g. "I like TV", "I like the gym." In small groups, or as a mingle, the students tell each other what they like doing in their free time.
   b) Keep the vocabulary work student-centred by boarding the pictures on page 36 and splitting the group into groups of 3 to identify the words. Alternatively, there are flash cards for this vocabulary in the Extra Materials section.
   c) The students can practise by telling each other which of the hobbies they like/dislike, e.g. "I like shopping, I don't like the gym."
   d) Pages 36-37 offer a chance to practise initial consonants.

   'Kim's game' is an excellent way to revise the vocabulary in your next class. Board the pictures and give the students a minute to memorise the words. After this time, take the images away and they try to recall the lexical set. Subsequent slides can include all the pictures except one ("Which picture is NOT here?").

2. I like Tik Tok, pages 38-40
   Aims: speaking, reading and writing

   a) Use pictures of 'Hong' and her interests to get the students interested in the topic.
   b) Get the group reading aloud, answering comprehension questions and finally, writing about their own hobbies. Encourage the stronger learners to extend their texts when writing about their free time. Including a LSCWC slot (page 40) will help prepare the learners for this writing task.
   c) The Workbook includes extra practice for these words: watch, like, go, see, the, we, gym, shopping, my. If you create flash cards for these, the learners will benefit from multiple exposures to the words. If time is short, this can always be done in your next class after the group reads the text again as revision.

3. I like shopping, pages 41-42
   Aim: phonics – 'ing' words

   a) The students have already seen a few 'ing' words in the vocabulary exercises and text about Hong. Mime some phrases with 'ing', e.g. "I like reading", "I don't like cleaning the kitchen" and then show the pictures on page 41 on the whiteboard. Pair the students up with the task, "What can you see?" In open-class feedback, personalise the vocabulary: "I like cooking, and you?"
   b) Board 'I like shopping' and clarify the 'ing' sound-spelling. There's no need to go into detail as regards the grammar - "we use 'ing' after 'like'" is sufficient.
   c) Test the students orally by dictating sentences, some with 'ing', some without. If they hear 'ing' they can show this by saying "Yes, i-n-g" or simply "No." If you prefer, they can clap if they hear 'ing' or shake their heads if there's no 'ing.' Here are some sentences you can use for this:
      1. I like shopping.
      2. I go to college every day.
      3. I don't like cleaning the kitchen.
      4. We speak English in class.
      5. I'm going home after class.
      6. We are reading and writing in class today.

7. I watch TV every day.
8. Do you like learning English?

d) Give the students further practice which features the written form. Initially, the students circle 'ing' words in the first exercise on page 42. After that they listen to you saying 6 more sentences, some with 'ing' words, some without and circle the 'ing' form if they hear it, for example:
    i. I went to a shop yesterday.
    ii. I like cooking.
    iii. I read every day.
    iv. We are writing in class now.
    v. I go swimming sometimes.
    vi. My son likes gaming.

e) Further personalisation could be given here by the students writing sentences about themselves, e.g. "I like cooking. I like shopping. I don't like gaming." Stronger learners could attempt their own 'ing' words, e.g. "I like playing football."

f) Plan revision for the following day through the students creating some 'ing' flash cards and/or a poster.

4. I am 18 years old, pages 43-45
   Aim: numeracy – numbers 10-20 in oral and numeric form

a) The initial matching task on page 43 puts the numbers into a context. If you have anyone aged 20 or under, ask "How old are you Suad?"

b) Focus orally on the numbers by asking the students to recite numbers 10-20 orally in pairs.

c) There are two controlled writing tasks to complete on page 43. Use the board or your finger in the air to model the formation of the numbers. Show the starting point of the pencil and the number of strokes to clarify.

d) Put the numbers into context for the 'listen and circle' task' on page 44, e.g.
    a. Our breaks are 15 minutes.
    b. My friend's son is 17 years old.
    c. I go to college by bike. It takes 20 minutes.
    d. My friend's daughter is 16 years old.

    e. I have my lunch at 12 o'clock.
    f. My son is 13 years old.

e) The controlled writing practice tasks on pages 44-45 could be done in class or set as homework.
f) For the final 'listen and write the number task', again, put the words into a context, e.g.
    a. I went to bed at 11 o'clock last night.
    b. My friend's son is 19 years old.
    c. I go to the city centre by bus. It takes 15 minutes.
    d. My friend's daughter is 14 years old.
    e. I have my morning break at 11 o'clock.
    f. My son is 13 years old.
    g. My car is 12 years old.
    h. I got a new t-shirt yesterday. It cost £15.
    i. I like my phone. The contract is £12 a month.
    j. In my morning class there are 18 students.

There are two activities in the Extra Materials section which can be used to revise these numbers: cut-out cards for numbers 10-20 and bingo.

5. Numbers, page 46
   Aim: numeracy (revision of numeric forms learnt so far)

While in unit 1, this end-of-unit task focused on initial consonants, in this case the group focuses on numeracy. The teacher asks the students to identify the different numeric forms, e.g. "1, which number is a postcode?" Suggested questions below:

a. A postcode?
b. A flat, part of an address?
c. A telephone number?
d. A bus number?
e. A date of birth?
f. A flat, part of an address?
g. A date of birth?
h. A postcode?
i. A telephone number?
j. A postcode?

6. Kahoot Quiz
   Aim: revision

   Finish the unit with a Kahoot quiz. Search 'TeacherGCC' (case specific) on Kahoot and look for the quiz for unit 2.

For a free Answer Key for every unit, visit www.esolbooks.com.

Unit 3: My day

Speaking/reading/writing: describing routines, describing your favourite day

Vocabulary: routines, days of the week

Numeracy: time-telling

Phonics: e and ee; ay; initial consonants – end-of-unit revision

Extra Material: Routines vocabulary flash cards; time-telling flash cards; days of the week flash cards

1. My day, pages 48-49
   Aims: vocabulary - hobbies and interests; phonics - initial consonants

   a) For the lead in, mime and drill some of the phrases from page 48, e.g. get up, brush my teeth, go to bed. Model the task by telling the class your routine before the students tell each other theirs in small groups.
   b) Board the pictures on page 48 and put the students into groups of 3 to identify the words. In open-class feedback, clarify the vocabulary and help with pronunciation by drilling the phrases.
   c) Pages 48-49 offer a chance to practise initial consonants.

2. My day, pages 50-53
   Aims: speaking, reading and writing

   a) Use pictures to introduce 'Ana' and elicit her routine from the group.
   b) The students read the text aloud and do the subsequent comprehension tasks. The error correction task on page 50 can be done orally beforehand (the learners shout "No!" when they hear a mistake).
   c) After the LSCWC task on page 53, the students write their routines and then employ the LSCWC method on their texts for further practice.

d) The Workbook includes Dolch List practice for these words: go, at, bed, have, get, watch, college, o'clock, finish. Plan a flash cards stage during this class, or the following day.

3. What's the time? Pages 54-57
Aim: numeracy – time-telling (o'clock and half past)

I have tried teaching more phrases than "It's one o'clock" and "It's half past one" / "It's one thirty" in one class previously and overwhelmed the learners so I have cut this back to initially just practising these three forms. Later in the year more complex language can be introduced. If your class is keen to go further, I have found that learners find "two forty-five" much easier than "quarter to three."

a) Introduce the context through personalised questions, e.g. "What time is it now? What time do you get up? What time do we start class?"
b) Take an analogue clock to class to clarify "It's one o'clock" and "It's half past one" / "It's one thirty."
c) Use the board to model the task on page 54 before students do this in pairs. Page 55 offers more practice. Flash cards are an excellent way to give students through practice of this language (there's a set in the Extra Materials section at the back of this book). Split the class into groups of three, give each group a dozen flash cards showing various times (see below) for them to ask each other, "What's the time?" Monitor to check they are telling the time correctly.

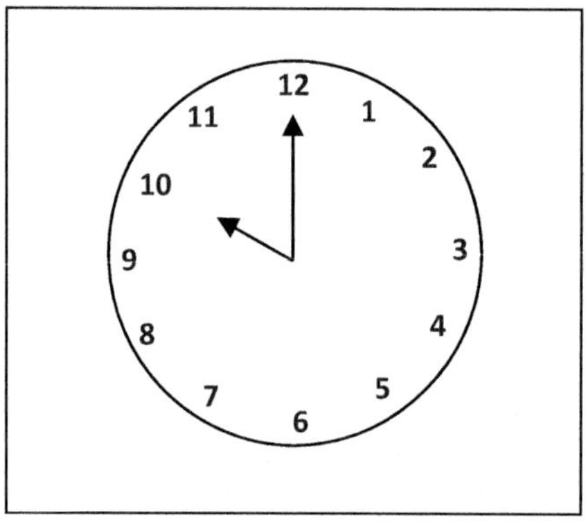

d) Page 56 includes practice of listening for and then writing the time. Firstly, the teacher dictates times for the students to circle the one they hear. Put the times in a short phrase to add context, e.g. "Number one, I have dinner at 6 o'clock", "number two, I get up at half past 7." Example sentences below:

1. I get up at 6 o'clock.
2. I have breakfast at half past 7.
3. I have a coffee at 11 o'clock.
4. I go home at half past 5.
5. I go to bed at 12 o'clock.

e) Repeat this for the subsequent task on the same page but this time the students write the time, using numeric form – choose your own times and put them into a context. There are some below for you to use / adapt.

a. My son starts school at 9 o'clock.
b. He has a morning break at half past 10.
c. He finishes at 3 o'clock.
d. I teach a morning class at half past 9.
e. I finish my morning class at 12 o'clock.
f. I cook dinner at 6 o'clock.
g. I eat dinner at 7 o'clock.
h. I watch TV at about 8 o'clock.
i. I went to bed at half past ten last night.
j. I get up at 8 o'clock at the weekend.

f) Page 57 personalises the language, combining time-telling with the vocabulary and phrases learnt previously in the unit.

4. Days, pages 58-60
   Aims: speaking, reading and writing

a) Set the context by asking the students which days they like/don't like. Model the speaking task ("I like Saturday. I play football with my son. I watch TV and eat ice cream") before the group chats in pairs/small groups about their favourite day.

b) Show pictures of 'Reza' and the activities he mentions to introduce the students to the main ideas in the text. The material offers the opportunity for the learners to read aloud and then do comprehension tasks.
e) The students focus on a day they like/don't like as the writing task.

5. Days, pages 61-62
   Aims: vocabulary – days of the week; phonics – 'ay'

   a) The context has already been set by the previous lesson about 'Reza.' Practise the days of the week orally, e.g. "How many days of the week are there? Which days do you go to college?" etc.
   b) Drill the seven days and do some further drills on this as a group by nominating individuals, e.g. Teacher: "Monday", Students: "Monday, Tuesday, Wednesday." Ramp this up if appropriate, e.g. "Which day is after Tuesday?", "Before Sunday?" etc.
   c) There are cards to order in the Extra Materials section before the students focus on spelling (page 61). Elicit that we always start these word with capital letters.
   d) Elicit other words with 'ay', e.g. day, say, today, May, pay. The students then circle 'ay' in the words at the top of page 64.
   e) The class copy the words into the diagram and then read the words aloud in pairs.
   f) If you have time, further practice through flash cards, a mind map and/or making a poster will be useful.

6. in/on/at, pages 63-64
   Aim: grammar - prepositions of time

   a) Use the students' routines to set the context, e.g. "Do we go to college in the morning or afternoon?", "When do you watch TV?" etc. Clarify the vocabulary: morning, afternoon, evening.
   b) You could try a diagnostic task here, e.g. instruct the students to tell each other their daily routines, including when they do each action, e.g. "I go to college in the afternoon, I have my dinner at 7 o'clock" etc. Board pictures to help (see the Power Point slides on www.esolbooks.com).
   c) Clarify the prepositions, *in* the morning/*at* 10:00/*on* Saturday.

d) Do the first task on page 63 as a group. Elicit the initial vowel sounds for the three prepositions. Note that these are more difficult for students than initial consonant sounds.
e) Sentences 1–7 on page 63 give the students reading and writing practice using the prepositions. Board the sentences and read them aloud before they do the tasks in the Student's Book.
f) Page 64 includes a table with phrases they can combine to write full sentences, e.g. I clean my flat every day, I go to college in the afternoon. Can the stronger learners write without using the table? Everyone can practise further by using LSCWC on the texts they have built.

7. e/ee, pages 65-67
   Aim: phonics – e and ee

   a) Introduce this practice of the two vowel sounds through pictures on the board of a bed and someone sleeping. Board the words 'bed' and 'sleep', elicit the sounds and clarify the difference: short sound versus long sound. Exaggerate the way we form the 'ee' sound with our mouths.
   b) Show the pictures from page 65 on the whiteboard for the learners to name the words in pairs and then drill the vocabulary in open-class feedback.
   c) Reinforce the sound-spelling link through a minimal pairs drill where the students can shout out "one e" or "double e." Use the words from the pictures you displayed on the board plus a few more, e.g. teeth, bed, sleep, three, pen, leg, tree, men, three, ten, pencil, red, sheep, get, knee.
   d) Pages 65-67 feature practice for the students of the words in their written form. The group can read the words in the table aloud in pairs after copying them into the correct column.

8. 'abc', page 68
   Aim: initial consonant sounds

   Suggested words below:

1. very	6. shower
2. don't	7. good
3. Wednesday	8. sofa
4. bed	9. car
5. time	10. now

9. Kahoot Quiz
   Aim: revision

   Finish the unit with a Kahoot quiz.

   A fun activity to include toward the end of the unit is to watch a video with the class. Students love Mr Bean and there's an excellent episode in which he is late for the dentist. During the episode he goes through his morning routine but in the usual crazy and chaotic way that Mr Bean is famous for! Go to www.esolbooks.com for a worksheet and instructions on how to exploit this in class.

For a free Answer Key for every unit, visit www.esolbooks.com.

Unit 4: I like the bus

Speaking/reading/writing: using transport

Vocabulary: transport

Phonics: revision of 'ing' (going to)

Numeracy: numbers 10-100 in numeric form

Extra Material: vehicles vocabulary flash cards; numbers 0-100 bingo

1. I like the bus, pages 70-71
   Aims: vocabulary – lexical set of vehicles

   a) Mime some vehicles to get the lesson off to a fun start, e.g. a bike, drive a car, a motorbike. Can the students name more vehicles?
   b) Board pictures of the vehicles for the learners to name them in pairs.
   c) The students draw upon initial consonants to fill in the gaps on page 70 and fast finishers can try the following page too.

2. I like the bus, pages 72-76
   Aims: speaking, reading and writing

   a) Ask the students, "How do you go to college? How many buses? How long does it take? Do you like the bus?" and drill useful phrases. They chat in small groups about this.
   b) Introduce 'Mohammad' and clarify how he gets to college as a precursor to the text.
   c) The students read the text aloud and do the comprehension tasks.
   d) The exercises on pages 74-76 can be used to prepare the group for the free writing task which follows.
   e) The learners write about how they go to college, using the text about Mohammad as a model. Plan the type of text/language they can use for this, e.g. "My name is Samira. I go to college by bus. I take one bus, the number 66. It takes 30 minutes.

I like the bus. The bus is very good." Fast finishers can write more, e.g. "I watch You Tube on the bus."

f) The Workbook includes Dolch List practice for these words from the text: go, by, two, bus, take, car, like, hour, one.

3. I take bus number 75, pages 77-79
   Aim: numeracy – numbers 10-100 in numeric form

   a) Page 77 exploits the context to introduce this numeracy class. Use this page as a diagnostic – can the learners identify the bus numbers? After that, drill numbers 10, 20, 30 up to 100. Write some more numbers on the board to see how good the students are with this, e.g. 31, 47, 58, 69 etc.
   b) Page 78 gives some practice of number formation.
   c) Page 79 pushes the learners a little more: for the first task ('listen and circle'), put the sentences into a short phrase, e.g.
      a. My best friend is 40 years old.
      b. My mum is 78 years old.
      c. I have 25p in my pocket.
      d. My friend John is 54 years old.
      e. When I was 20 years old I was living in London.

   For the final exercise, choose numbers appropriate to the level of the class, e.g. if the students have found this difficult just dictate numbers such as 20, 40, 55 etc. If they've coped well, then push them with a more difficult range, e.g. 67, 23, 49 etc. Play bingo for further practice (cards in the Extra Materials section).

4. She's going to the city centre, pages 80-81
   Aims: grammar – going to for future plans; phonics – 'ing' (revision)

   a) Before focusing on the language, show the pictures from page 80 for the students to discuss in pairs ("Where are they?"). In open-class feedback, ask, "Who is going to India by plane? Picture one? Two? Three? Who is going to the city centre by bus?" etc. The learners match the images to the phrases.

b) Clarify that 'going to' refers to the future. Ask the students, "Where are you going after college?" and drill some useful phrases. The students can repeat this in small groups to talk about 'after college' and 'tomorrow.'
c) Consider a substitution drill, e.g. Teacher: "college", student: "I'm going to college tomorrow." Teacher: "the gym", student: "I'm not going to the gym tomorrow."
d) Write one of the phrases from page 80 on the board to highlight 'ing.' You could add a brief minimal pairs task here where the teacher dictates a sentence and the students say, "every day" or "tomorrow", e.g. Teacher: "I get up at 6 o'clock", students: "every day." Teacher: "I'm going shopping", students: "tomorrow." For further speaking practice the group can discuss their future plans for 'after college', 'tomorrow' and 'on Saturday.'
e) The material provides literacy practice of the language. The students use the table on page 81 to write personalised sentences. Stronger students can try to write their own sentences. Finally, everyone can use LSCWC to write their sentences again without copying.

5. abc, page 82
   Aim: phonics - initial consonant sounds

   Suggested words below:

1. van	6. never
2. taxi	7. please
3. do	8. sing
4. car	9. went
5. train	10.kind

6. Kahoot Quiz
   Aim: revision

   Finish the unit with a Kahoot quiz.

For a free Answer Key for every unit, visit www.esolbooks.com.

Unit 5: My city

Speaking/reading/writing: describing a town/city; describing your home

Vocabulary: places in a town/city

Phonics: the /k/ sound (words beginning with 'c'/'k'); initial consonants – end-of-unit revision

Numeracy: saying and writing years; revision of various numerical forms covered so far

Extra Material: places in a town/city vocabulary flash cards; years flash cards

1. My city, pages 84-85
   Aims: vocabulary - lexical set of places in a town; phonics - initial consonants

   a) Show pictures of the vocabulary on page 84 and put the students into small groups to identify the words. Alternatively, use the flash cards in the Extra Materials section.
   b) The students can practise by telling each other which of the places they go to every day/sometimes.
   c) Pages 84-85 offer the learners a chance to focus on initial consonants.
   d) If time, the group can write the sentences they used earlier, e.g. "I go to the shops every day. I go to the gym sometimes."

2. My city, pages 86-88
   Aims: speaking, reading and writing

   a) As a lead in, chat about the town/city where the students live, e.g. "Do you like Glasgow? What do you like?" Model the task by telling them what you like before the learners chat in small groups.
   b) Use pictures of aspects of Glasgow mentioned in the text, such as the rain and the parks, to help the group predict its contents.
   c) Pages 86-88 include the text the students read aloud and comprehension tasks.

d) The LSCWC task on page 88 sets the learners up for the final task during which they write about their own town/city.

Assuming you don't live in Glasgow, consider adapting this text and tasks for your group's context.

3. c/k, pages 89-91

   Aim: phonics – words beginning 'c' or 'k' with the hard /k/ sound

   The staging for this is a little different to previous phonics lessons as this time the students focus on a single sound with two different spellings. As the previous technique of students listening and distinguishing two different sounds doesn't apply, note the change in staging below.

   a) For the oral work, ask the students, "Do you like college?" and drill the phrase "I like college." After boarding this phrase, focus on the 'c' in college and the 'k' in like to elicit the sound for the spellings of these two letters and emphasise that it's the same sound but two different letters. Ask the students if they know any more words beginning with 'c' or 'k'. Drill some of these words.
   b) Show the pictures from page 89 on the whiteboard before pairing the students up with the task, "What can you see?" Drill the words in open-class feedback.
   c) The group attempts the matching task on page 89. It's worth clarifying that we have more words beginning with c than with k. The following page helps them to group these words.
   d) Now the students have seen the written form, they are ready for a 'minimal pairs' task in an open-class stage. Say the words from page 89 and the students call out 'c' or 'k' (as in the pronunciation of the letters, /si:/ or /keɪ/ rather than the sounds). Add other relevant vocabulary the learners know, including their classmates' names/countries if applicable. The group can also read aloud words displayed on the whiteboard (prepare slides with a single word on each slide). Do this as a class and then nominate individuals.
   e) Page 91 is the final practice task to assess how well the students have done with this.

f) Revise this through homework tasks in the Workbook and revision the following day, e.g. flash cards/mind maps/dictation (say ten words and the students write 'c' or 'k' for each one - stronger students attempt to write the full word).

The students will quite possibly think of some words which are spelt with c/k but with a different sound, e.g. city, chicken. It's good for learners to know that letters often have different sounds ("Yes, 'letter c' has many sounds, maybe /k/ but maybe /s/ or /tʃ/") but keep them on track with the phonics of this class: "Today we're just looking at 'c' and 'k' for the /k/ sound." Introducing 'soft c' at this stage may well be overwhelming for your weaker learners so I wouldn't spend too much time on this.

4. My flat, pages 92-95
   Aims: speaking, reading and writing

   a) Introduce the topic with some chat about the students' homes, e.g. "Do you live in a flat or a house? Do you like your flat? Do you like your neighbours? Why/ why not?" Model the task before the students speak to each other about their flat/house. As a pre-reading task, use pictures to focus the students on 'Asma' and the contents of the text.
   b) The material includes a text for the students to read aloud and comprehension tasks, after which they write about their own home and neighbours. The tasks on pages 94 and 95 help the class build up for the final writing task.
   c) The Workbook includes Dolch List practice for these words: like, have, my, live, people, the, flat, city, in, don't. Plan a flash cards stage during this class, or the following day.

5. My flat, page 96
   Aim: writing your address

   This is a chance for the class to revise an area from unit 1. Hopefully the students will have remembered most/all of their addresses.

6. 2020, pages 97-101
   Aim: saying and writing years

   a) If you teach groups of asylum seekers / refugees, as a lead in to this lesson, ask the learners when they came to the UK (or the country in which you teach). Drill the phrase 'I came to (the UK) in (2020) and put the students into small groups to compare.

b) Pages 97-98 continue this context for the students. The students saw Asma in an earlier unit so ask a few questions about her before the group reads the text aloud and attempts the comprehension tasks. This concludes with a brief writing task for the learners on page 98.

c) The following page is a matching task to introduce other years. Show the pictures on the board without the years to start with. What do the group know about these people/events? You will need to clarify some of these for them, e.g. women's fight to vote in elections in the UK (see below for the answers).

d) Test the students: can they say these years and match the events to when they happened? Let this run for a few minutes before clarifying how we break this down ("nineteen...eighty-three"). Monitor to give clues for these events, e.g. "When did we have the first mobile phone? When did You Tube start?" The focus here is on saying the years correctly so help the students by asking questions for them to give short answers, e.g. "Samira, When did Tok Tok start?" If you can play You Tube videos in class then a few of these might help the students to understand the events. Clarify the answers in open-class feedback:

    1. Tik Tok started in 2017.
    2. Shops sold mobile phones for the first time in 1983.
    3. The first car was in 1886.
    4. The first You Tube video was in 2005.
    5. The first camera was in 1816.
    6. We first time we went to the moon was in 1969.
    7. The first football World Cup was in 1930.

e) Page 100 continues to focus receptively on the years. Put the language into a context here, e.g.

    a. I was living in London in 2000.
    b. I moved to London in 1997.
    c. My brother was born in 1973.
    d. You Tube started in 2009.
    e. Asma came to the UK in 2020.
    f. The first football World Cup was in 1930.
    g. I moved to Scotland in 2005.

    h. I went to Spain on holiday in 2021.

f) The first task on page 101 provides practice of number formation.

g) The final task is more difficult. Again, put the years into a context, e.g.
    a. Ali (or another student in the class) started college in (2022).
    b. Zbida (or another student) came to the UK in (2019).
    c. My best friend moved to the UK in 2010.
    d. I was born in 1975.
    e. I learnt to drive in 1993.
    f. bought my first car in 2008.
    g. I got a new bike in 2022.
    h. My brother was born in 1970.
    i. Nelson Mandella was born in 1928.
    j. Barack Obama was born in 1961.

h) Set the students up to write some personalised sentences using years, e.g.
I came to the UK in (2019).
I started at this college in (2022).
I got my phone in (2022).

If you know students have children, they could also write about them, e.g.
My daughter was born in (2009).

Look in the Extra Materials section for flash cards to further practise this language.

7. Q and A, pages 102-104
Aim: revision of numerical forms covered so far

a) Display a picture of Mohammad and see what the students can remember about him (he's first seen in unit 1).
b) Model the matching task on page 102 and let the students try it without too much help. Step in after a few minutes to help.
c) Show the students pictures of Kate and Willie. See if they can guess their ages. Tell them where they live and when they came to London/Cardiff.

d) Display the text on page 103 on the board and read it aloud. Either tell the students about Willie and Kate or go to www.esolbooks.com to access an audio recording. Here is the missing information: Kate: 26 years old; Tel number: 0770 090 0991; Flat 1/1, 52 High Street, London N1 8PK; I came to London in 2020. Willie: 34 years old; Tel number: 029 2018 0985; Flat 3/1, 88 New Road, Cardiff CF10 1AE, I came to Cardiff in 2018.
e) The lesson finishes with a personalised writing task on page 104.

8. Numbers, page 105
   Aim: numeracy (revision)

   This end-of-unit task The teacher asks the students to identify the different numerical forms, e.g. "1, which number is a postcode?" Suggested questions below:

   a. A postcode?
   b. A flat, part of an address?
   c. A telephone number?
   d. A bus number?
   e. A date of birth?
   f. A flat, part of an address?
   g. A date of birth?
   h. A postcode?
   i. A telephone number?
   j. A postcode?

9. Kahoot Quiz
   Aim: revision

   Finish the unit with a Kahoot quiz.

For a free Answer Key for every unit, visit www.esolbooks.com.

Unit 6: Food

Speaking/reading/writing: describing food, describing mealtimes; punctuation – using capital letters and full stops

Speaking and listening - ordering food in a cafe

Vocabulary: food, mealtimes

Numeracy: numbers 1 – 100; prices and giving change

Phonics: split digraphs ('magic e')

Extra Material: Food vocabulary flash cards; prices flash cards

1. Food, pages 108-109
   Aims: vocabulary – food; phonics – initial consonant sounds

   a) As a lead in, tell the students which food you like/don't like before they chat about their favourite food and drink in small groups.
   b) Board the pictures from page 108 or distribute pictures on cards (you can find flash cards in the Extra Materials section at the back of this book) for the students to work together to name the food. Clarify and drill the words in open-class feedback. The class can chat in groups for further practice, e.g. "I like chocolate, I don't like carrots."
   c) The students use the initial consonant sounds to help them fill in the gaps on pages 108-109.

2. Food, pages 110-113
   Aims: Speaking, reading and writing

   a) Ask, "What do people eat and drink in the UK?" and board pictures of the food and drink mentioned in the text.
   b) The material enables practice of reading aloud and comprehension tasks.
   c) The students speak about their favourite food and drink and popular food in their countries and then write a short text about this. You can include the controlled

writing practice tasks on page 112 as a bridge between the speaking task and free writing practice.

d) The Workbook includes Fry/Dolch List practice of these words from the text: eat, like, have, rice, food, drink, snack, dinner, chicken.

3. Food, page 114
Aim: vocabulary – fruit/vegetable/meat/drinks

a) Provide plenty of context through pictures of the food on page 114 displayed on the whiteboard (slides available on www.esolbooks.com). Clarify and drill the words in open-class feedback.
b) Use the pictures to clarify the vocabulary, e.g. "Is a banana a vegetable? Meat? Fruit?" Check understanding by dictating types of food for the students to classify, e.g. Teacher: "carrots?", students: "vegetable." The learners can repeat this task in pairs.
c) Read the words on page 114 aloud for the students and model the categorising task before the class writes the words into the correct columns.

4. Food, pages 115-117
Aims: speaking, reading and writing

a) Board pictures of popular food eaten for breakfast and dinner and as snacks. After the students work in groups to name the food, elicit the vocabulary above and get them chatting about what they eat for breakfast and dinner and which snacks they like. Drill useful language beforehand, e.g. "I have breakfast at 6 o'clock. I like coffee and cereal."
b) Introduce 'Jo' and clarify what she likes eating before showing the students the text.
c) Read the text aloud chorally and then the students read it aloud in pairs. Some reading comprehension tasks follow the text.
d) The learners write about their preferences for breakfast, snacks and dinner. Encourage the stronger students to write as much as possible.

5. Sam's café, pages 118-121, for the audio go to www.esolbooks.com.
Aims: numeracy – saying and writing prices, adding up prices, calculating change; listening and speaking – ordering in cafes

a) Ask the students if they go to cafes or restaurants, what they eat and drink there and which restaurants they like. They discuss the pictures in pairs and guess the prices of the different snacks and drinks on page 118. Do this as a diagnostic task (can they say prices in English?).
b) Clarify the coins and notes found in the UK (or the country in which you teach). Use realia or board a picture of various coins to clarify 'pence' and 'pounds.' You could ask the students to put some money on the table to name. Pair the students up to say the prices at the bottom of page 118.
c) Elicit the word 'menu' and then display the menu on page 119 on the board. Read it aloud for the students and ask questions such as "How much is tea?" The students repeat this in pairs, e.g. "How much is ice cream?", "£3."
d) Either set the questions on page 119 orally or display them on the board and read them aloud. The audio is on www.esolbooks.com.
e) After checking the answers, play the recording again, pausing after a useful phrase (e.g. "Can I have a burger and chips please?") and ask, "What did he say?" Repeat this for other phrases.
f) Nominate a student to help you model a role play, feeding in other useful phrases you feel appropriate. The students take turns as customer and cafe worker. Use the menu on page 119 for this but encourage them to ask for something which is not on the menu. The more inventive comical members of the class usually have some fun with this, while practising some useful functional English.
g) Focus on the idea of calculating change by using some realia such as a £5 note. For example, say "I buy a coffee for £3 and I give £5" while handing the money to a student. Ask, "What does he give me?" Elicit "£2 change." The students do the same task but using the prices and food and drink on the menu. Finally, they do a similar task but this time incorporating some reading practise through the 7 questions on page 120.
h) The next task on page 120 helps the students practise number formation as well as writing the pound symbol. You could adapt this if you are teaching outside the UK, of course, with a worksheet featuring your home currency. Model the formation of the numbers and pound sign on the board or using your finger in the air. Emphasise where the pencil starts and finishes though if the students can write a number successfully with their own method then that's fine with me!
i) The 'Listen and circle' task on page 121 gives the students some receptive practice of prices. Put the prices into a short phrase, e.g.
    a. I have £10 in my pocket.

b. I spent £25 in the supermarket yesterday.
c. I went to a café on Saturday and my coffee and cake cost £6.50.
d. I went to the shop and got a drink. They gave me 20p change.
e. I got a new t-shirt yesterday. It cost £9.99.
f. My son's bike cost £95.

j) The subsequent 'Listen and write the price' task on page 121 is more productive. Again, put the prices into a short phrase, e.g.

a. I spent £30 in the supermarket yesterday.
b. I got a new pair of shoes yesterday for £19.99.
c. I went to a café on Sunday with my family and the food and drinks cost £15.
d. I went to the supermarket yesterday and got a drink and a snack. After I paid, they gave me 50p change.
e. I got a new t-shirt yesterday. It cost £4.99.
f. My watch cost £8.99.
g. You can buy a coffee in my favourite café for £3.50.
h. I went to the barber at the weekend. My hair cut cost £12.
i. I got a new bag yesterday. It cost £14.99.
j. I went to a café on Saturday. I got a cup of tea. It cost £2.75.

Adapt the prices above for your group if they seem too easy/difficult. After checking the answers as a group, pair the learners up to read the prices aloud for more practice. There's a further practice task for this area in the Extra Materials section.

6. Chilli, pages 122-124
Aims: speaking, reading and writing

a) Show pictures representing the story of when my son mistook chilli sauce for orange juice! Pictures of Isaac, eggs and chilli sauce will do as a pre-reading task. After the learners name the vocabulary shown in the images, tell the story. Students usually find the idea of a toddler drinking chilli sauce quite amusing!
b) The text to read aloud and comprehension tasks follow.
c) This material doesn't lead to a personalised writing task but you could ask the learners to reform the text in their own words, as a group (the LEA model). Sometimes students add their own spin, e.g. "It's a funny story."

Do you have a good story to tell? You could follow the same steps above and create your own worksheet.

7. I like rice, pages 125-126
   Aims: phonics – 'magic e' (long i sound + consonant + e)

   a) Use pictures of rice and wine to link the context of food with the phonics work. Clarify the long i (/aɪ/) and silent letter (no /e/ sound for letter 'e') in these words.
   b) Display the pictures from page 125 on the whiteboard for the students to name them in pairs. Drill the words in open-class feedback.
   c) Board a few words from the task, for example:

      rice
      wine
      time
      drive

      Elicit that they all include the letters 'i' and 'e'. Drill the words in a group of three to emphasise that they rhyme, for example, "rice, wine, time."
   d) The students match the words to pictures (page 125) and then attempt to write the words on page 126.
   e) Flash cards/Kim's game will help the students revise this phonics the following day.

8. abc, page 127
   Aim: phonics - initial consonant sounds

   Suggested words below:

   1. drive
   2. chilli
   3. wine
   4. breakfast
   5. like
   6. mango
   7. potatoes
   8. vegetable
   9. carrots
   10. tea

9. Kahoot Quiz
   Aim: revision

For a free Answer Key for every unit, visit www.esolbooks.com.

Unit 7: The Weather

Speaking/reading/writing: the weather

Vocabulary: the weather; the months

Phonics: vowel sounds (o, i, u)

Extra Material: Weather vocabulary flash cards; months of the year flash cards

1. The weather, pages 130-131
   Aims: vocabulary – the weather; phonics - initial consonants

   a) Start by asking, "How's the weather today?" Mime various weather conditions, e.g. "It's cold", "It's hot", "It's raining."
   b) Keep the vocabulary work student-centred by boarding the pictures on page 130 and splitting the group into groups of 3 to identify the words.
   c) Pages 130-131 offer a chance to practise initial consonants.

2. Months, pages 132-134
   Aims: vocabulary – the months; phonics - initial consonants

   a) Ask the students some questions to give the language some context, e.g. "What's the month now?", "When is your birthday?", "When do we start college? When do we finish?" See if the students can recite the months in order and then drill the months in chunks of three ("January, February, March"). Put the learners into pairs to repeat this.
   b) Pages 132-134 give the students a chance to practise initial consonants and spelling. Elicit that these begin with a capital letter and help the students notice the rime, '-ember' of three months.

3. Manchester, pages 135-138
   Aims: Speaking, reading and writing

   a) Ask the students to discuss the weather in both the city where they live and their home country, in groups of 3.
   b) Ask if anyone knows Manchester. Ask, "How's the weather?" If necessary, tell the students about this city. Show a picture of Amy on page 135 and summarise her opinion of this city.
   c) The students can read the text aloud, firstly as a group and then in pairs.
   d) An error correction task follows. Do this orally first and then the students can read to find the mistakes.
   e) Further reading and writing practice follows on page 136.
   f) There's some controlled practice on the subsequent page before the students write about the weather in the place they live now and their own country.

4. Aim: phonics – short vowel sounds in CVC words, pages 139-142

   a) See if the students can fill in the gaps for themselves in the three words on page 139 before clarifying the sound-spelling combinations. Elicit the sound related to each letter and then bring in more context by displaying the images on page 140 on the board, without any text. After clarifying the vocabulary, ask the students which of the three vowels the words include. Board the three letters and ask, "dog, letter i, o or u?" The learners can reply by saying "letter o" / "letter i" / "letter u."
   b) Consolidate the work done orally with the gap-fill on page 140 and the matching task on page 142.
   c) The final task on page 142 pushes the students to write the full word. Help the weaker students in monitoring by saying the words for them to listen for the sounds. Also, allow anyone struggling to have a quick look at the previous page to help.

5. abc, page 143
   Aim: phonics - initial consonant sounds

   Suggested words below:

   1. very
   2. chair
   3. weather
   4. cold
   5. years
   6. sit
   7. rain
   8. where
   9. shower
   10. time

6. Kahoot Quiz
   Aim: revision

   Finish the unit with a Kahoot quiz. Search 'TeacherGCC' (case specific) on Kahoot and look for the quiz for unit 7.

For a free Answer Key for every unit, visit www.esolbooks.com.

Unit 8: Happy days

Speaking/reading/writing: describing special occasions

Vocabulary: Christmas; months (revision)

Phonics: y as final letter (/i:/)

Numeracy: dates and ordinal numbers

Extra Material: Christmas vocabulary flash cards

1. Happy Christmas! Pages 146-147
   Aims: vocabulary – Christmas; phonics – initial consonants

   a) Put the students into small groups to discuss what happens at Christmas. Show the pictures from page 146 as a prompt, if necessary.
   b) Board the pictures from that page or use the flash cards from the Extra Materials section and give the learners a chance to name them. Clarify the vocabulary and help with pronunciation during open-class feedback.
   c) As the students write the first letter(s) on page 146, monitor to say the words so that they can listen for the initial consonant sound. In open-class feedback, highlight the 'ch' in 'Christmas.' Elicit that 'ch' is usually the /tʃ/ sound, as in 'chicken' but clarify that for one spelling we can have more than one sound. If you think your students are of a high enough level, you could spend some time on this, for example, by eliciting some other words with 'ch' words with a /k/ sound, e.g. chemist, mechanic, school, stomach, headache. This is advanced phonics, however, and there aren't so many words with 'ch' pronounced /k/ so keep it brief.

2. Happy Christmas! Pages 148-151
   Aims: Speaking, reading and writing

   a) The vocabulary work leads nicely onto this text about Christmas in the UK.
   b) The material includes the text for students to read aloud and subsequent comprehension tasks.

c) A writing task could be to write a brief summary of the text or you could open up a discussion about similar events in the students' countries such as Eid.
d) The Workbook includes Dolch List practice for these words from the text: at, eat, big, buy, give, have, happy, children.

3. Happy New Year! Pages 152-154
   Aims: Speaking, reading and writing

   a) Elicit the phrase 'Happy New Year!" and ask the students what happens in the UK and in their countries at New Year. Speak briefly as a class and get the group chatting about this in small groups.
   b) The students read the text aloud and do the subsequent comprehension tasks.
   c) Finally, the group speaks and then writes about New Year in the UK/their countries.

4. Happy Birthday! Pages 155-157
   Aims: speaking, reading and writing

   a) Elicit the phrase 'Happy Birthday!' and ask the students how they celebrate. Encourage them to chat in small groups and help with vocabulary. They'll almost definitely mention the ideas in the text, e.g. a party, a cake. Introduce the ideas in the text in open-class feedback.
   b) The students read the text aloud and then do the comprehension tasks on page 155 followed by the gap-fill on the following page.
   c) The LSCWC prepares the learners for the final writing task in which they write about how they celebrate their birthdays.

5. Happy Birthday! No material – use the board and flash cards
   Aims: phonics - final 'y' (/i:/)

   a) Focus on 'happy' in 'Happy birthday!" Ask the class, "Can you hear the /i:/ sound?" Board the word and clarify the sound-spelling link and that this is used for words which finish 'y.' Clarify that 'y' at the beginning of words is different (/j/ as in 'yes'). The 'ay' rime in 'birthday' is an exception here and also words like 'my' but don't mention these at all or at least not at this stage, instead referring to it after highlighting final y, if at all.

b) Elicit other words which finish with 'y' and write them on the board in a mind map, e.g. baby, body, very, twenty, many, family, funny, party, dirty. Read the words aloud.
c) The students can copy them into their notebooks and then read aloud in pairs. Further practice is possible through flash cards and a classroom poster.

6. Dates, pages 158-165

   Aims: Vocabulary revision – months; Numeracy – saying, reading and writing dates

   a) Show a picture of Mohammad and see if the students can remember anything about him. The initial task on page 158 features the target language in context.
   b) The students tick day/month/year for each of the numbers. As a brief diagnostic, ask some of your younger learners their dates of birth.
   c) Revise the months orally before the students attempt the gap-fill on page 159.
   d) Introduce the target language of ordinal numbers by displaying Mohammed's date of birth on the board and asking, "How do we say this?" Drill the word 'first' before setting the students up with the matching task on page 160. Help with the pronunciation of the ten ordinal numbers during feedback and elicit that 'th' is the most common ending for these. Page 161 gives the group the chance to practice.
   e) The lesson gives more practice of saying, reading and writing dates through the context of various individuals' dates of birth. Start by boarding pictures of the people and asking the learners if they they can guess their ages. They then match the people to their dates of birth. The answers are on page 163 and also below:

Jo	Mohammad	Willie	Amina	Lisa
04.09.1999	01.03.2005	18.07.1991	20.02.60	03.01.2008

   f) There's a reading task on page 163 to help the learners to get used to the date format.

g) The 'listen and circle' task on page 164 gives some receptive practice for this language before some more difficult productive tasks on page 165. Put the dates into a context for the final task, for example:

   a. Barack Obama became US president on the 20th of January 2009.
   b. My best friend was born on the 1st of February 1980.
   c. Today's date is .....
   d. The next holiday will start on....
   e. The first time we went to the moon was on the 20th of July 1969.
   f. The first You Tube video was on the 14th of February 2005.
   g. Our first class this year was on ....
   h. We finish college this year on ....

7. abc, page 166
   Aim: phonics - initial consonant sounds

   Suggested words below:

1. very	6. make
2. today	7. good
3. happy	8. small
4. cards	9. was
5. your	10.new

8. Kahoot Quiz
   Aim: revision

   Finish the unit with a Kahoot quiz. Search 'TeacherGCC' (case specific) on Kahoot and look for the quiz for unit 8.

For a free Answer Key for every unit, visit www.esolbooks.com.

Unit 9: My flat

Speaking/reading/writing: describing your flat/house and possessions

Vocabulary: rooms in a flat/house, furniture

Numeracy: numbers 1 – 10 in written form

Phonics: 's' for plural nouns, o and oo

Extra Material: Furniture and household appliances vocabulary flash cards; numbers 1-10 flash cards (written form); numbers 1-10 bingo (written form)

1. Rooms, page 168
   Aim: vocabulary – rooms; phonics - initial consonant sounds

   a) Elicit the names of some rooms in a flat/house before drilling some short phrases, e.g. "I cook in the kitchen."
   b) Page 168 gives some practice of initial consonant sounds.

2. My flat, pages 169-171
   Aims: Speaking, reading and writing

   a) Model the task for the lead in, e.g. "I live in a flat. I have 3 bedrooms. I like the living room. I watch TV in the living room." etc. Drill some phrases before putting the learners into small groups to talk about their flat/house. As a pre-reading task, use pictures of 'Dave' and his flat to set the students up for the text.
   b) After reading the text aloud and doing the comprehension tasks, the group can speak about their house/flat again (change partners or run a mingle to keep it fresh), prepare towards the final task through a LSCWC stage and then write about their flat/house.
   c) The Workbook includes Dolch list practice for these words from the text: like, have, the, and, go, live, my, room, flat. Plan a flash cards stage during this class, or the following day.

3. My flat, pages 172-173
   Aim: vocabulary - furniture

   a) Ask the students, "What do you have in your living room? A sofa? A TV?" and then divide them into small groups to talk about what they have in each room.
   b) Show pictures of the furniture on page 172 on the whiteboard and let the students try to name the objects. Alternatively, use the flash cards in the Extra Materials section.
   c) They match these words that they now know in their oral form to the written form (page 172).
   d) For further practice, ask "Where is the TV?" (Students: "In the living room") and run this task in pairs. They then add the words to the correct columns on page 173.

4. 1, 2, 3, pages 174-175
   Aim: numeracy – numbers 1–10 in written form

   a) Introduce the context by asking, "How many chairs in this room? How many tables? How many students?" Revise numbers one to ten orally, if necessary.
   b) The students match the pictures to the phrases on page 174.
   c) Use the cut-out cards of the numbers from one to ten , in their written form from the Extra Materials section.
   d) The second task on page 174 gives the students some practice of initial consonant sounds. The words 'one' and 'two' are highly irregular so it's worth eliciting the /w/ sound in 'one' and the silent 'w' in 'two.'
   e) Page 175 gives further practice of writing the numbers.

5. I have three bedrooms, page 176
   Aims: grammar - singular and plural nouns; phonics - use of 's' for countable plural nouns; write about furniture and rooms in your flat

   a) Use some objects in the room to establish the context. For example, find two pencils and ask, "How many pencils?" Clarify the use of 's' for plural nouns and use the board to clarify the addition of an 's'. Emphasise the sound-spelling link.
   b) Practise with other items in the room, e.g. "How many students today?" This can be done as a class and repeated in pairs.

c) Page 176 provides reading/writing practice.
d) Personalise the language through a speaking and then writing task. Firstly, the students discuss their flat using numbers and 's' if necessary, e.g. "I live in a flat, I have three bedrooms, I have a sofa, I have two chairs in the living room." They then write this into a short text.

6. My caravan, pages 177-178
Aim: reading

a) As a lead in, show pictures of Ben and his caravan and ask if people have caravans in the students' countries.
b) Incorporate a pre-reading task: put the students into small groups to guess which rooms/furniture you can see in caravans. Clarify in open-class feedback which rooms Ben's caravan has.
c) The material gives the students the opportunity to read aloud and do the comprehension tasks.
d) This text doesn't lead on naturally to a personalised writing task. However, if the group seems interested in the topic, you could help them construct a LEA text, e.g. "We are speaking about caravans today. In a caravan you have a bedroom, a kitchen and a toilet. Caravans are very good."

7. o/oo, pages 179-180
Aim: phonics – o and oo

a) Show the pictures from page 179 on the whiteboard for the students to name them in pairs. Drill the words in open-class feedback.
b) Choose two of the pictures to clarify the difference between the vowel sounds, for example, a bedroom and a pot. Board the words, elicit the sounds and clarify the difference: short sound versus long sound. Exaggerate the way we form the 'oo' sound with our rounded mouths.
c) Reinforce the sound-spelling link through a minimal pairs drill where the students can shout out "one o" or "double o" while holding up one or two fingers. Use the words from the pictures plus a few more, e.g. room, pot, spoon, not, moon, pool, hot, dog, bedroom, hot, bathroom, mop, food, living room, on.
d) The material features reading and writing practice. The students can read the words in the table aloud after copying them into the correct column.

8. Numbers, page 181
   Aim: numeracy (revision)

   The teacher asks the students to identify the different numerical forms, e.g. "1, which number is a postcode?" Suggested questions below:

   a. A postcode?
   b. A year?
   c. A flat, part of an address?
   d. A bus number?
   e. A date of birth?
   f. A flat, part of an address?
   g. A date of birth?
   h. A postcode?
   i. A year?
   j. A telephone number?

9. Kahoot Quiz
   Aim: revision

   Finish the unit with a Kahoot quiz. Search 'TeacherGCC' (case specific) on Kahoot and look for the quiz for unit 9.

For a free Answer Key for every unit, visit www.esolbooks.com.

Unit 10: My country

Speaking/reading/writing: describing countries, punctuation – using capital letters (especially for cities and countries) and full stops

Vocabulary: countries and continents; colours

Numeracy: describing populations in millions

Phonics: ee and oo

Extra Material: colours vocabulary flash cards

1. My country, pages 184-186
   Aims: listening – world quiz; vocabulary – countries, flags, continents; phonics - initial consonant sounds; punctuation – use of capital letters for countries and continents; Writing – countries and continents

   a) Start with a quiz to kick off the topic. Ask students the questions below - they can work in pairs and write their answers, which are just a single letter each time. You can display the answer options on the whiteboard if you like or keep it purely oral.

      Q1: Where is Scotland? a) Africa b) Asia <u>c) Europe</u>
      Q2: Where is Sudan? <u>a) Africa</u> b) Asia c) Europe
      Q3: Where is China? a) Africa <u>b) Asia</u> c) Europe
      Q4: What is the biggest country in the world? a) China b) the US <u>c) Russia</u>
      Q5: How many people live in China? a) 10 million b) 500 million <u>c) 1.4 billion</u>
      Q6: How many people are in the world? a) 1 billion <u>b) 8 billion</u> c) 12 billion
      Q7-10: Show some of the flags on page 88 and ask, "Which country is this?"
      Q7: Show the Scottish flag. <u>a) Scotland</u> b) England c) France
      Q8: Show the Chinese flag. a) the US b) Brazil <u>c) China</u>
      Q9: Show the Canadian flag. a) Brazil b) the US <u>c) Canada</u>
      Q10: Show the Sudanese flag. <u>a) Sudan</u> b) South Africa c) India

   b) Show the pictures of the flags from page 184 on the whiteboard for the students to name in pairs.

c) Page 184 provides practice of initial consonants. Let the students start the task without reminding them to use capital letters for countries and see how they get on. Stop the class to revise this if most of the students have forgotten.
d) Clarify the continents 'Asia', 'Africa', 'Europe.' Model a question-answer practice task ("Where is Sudan?" – "Sudan is in Africa") before the students repeat this in pairs.
e) Page 186 provides practice of reading and writing using this language, culminating in the group writing about some of these countries, e.g. Sudan is in Africa. England is in Europe.

2. Scotland, pages 187-189
Aims: speaking, reading and writing

a) Lead into the topic by asking some questions about Scotland, e.g. "Where is Scotland? How many people live in Scotland?" Put them into groups to talk about this. In open-class feedback help the students with the language and pronunciation, e.g. "Scotland is in Europe. 5 million people live in Scotland." Try a substitution drill, e.g. Teacher: "Europe", student: "Scotland is in Europe." They can change partners and talk about Scotland again to practise.
b) Read the text aloud as a group and then the learners read aloud in pairs before trying the comprehension tasks on pages 187-188.
c) The students speak about their own countries and then write this as a brief text. There's a LSCWC task on page 189 to set them up for this. You will need to go online to check the populations of their countries.
d) The Workbook includes Dolch List practice for these words from the text: live, from, in, city, flag, speak, and, million, country, people. Plan a flash cards stage during this class, or the following day.

If you're teaching in a different country it would make sense to adapt this text for your own context, if you have time to create a worksheet.

3. Colours, pages 190-191
Aim: vocabulary – colours; phonics – initial consonants

Board some of the students' countries' flags (or the ones from page 184) and elicit the colours. After helping with pronunciation, check by nominating individuals to ask questions such as, "What colour is Scotland's flag?" Repeat this task with the students in pairs with a variation: one student describes a flag without saying the country for their group to identify, e.g. "The flag is red and white, which country?" The material provides reading and writing practice using the vocabulary. You could add a writing task: "I live in Scotland. Scotland's flag is blue and white. I am from Iran. Iran's flag is red, white and green."

4. Countries of the world, pages 192-194
   Aims: listening, speaking and writing

   a) Show pictures which represent the six countries and ask, "Which country is this? Where is it? What's the capital city?" Put the students into small groups to share information about the countries.
   b) Include a listening stage where you describe one of the countries for the students to identify, e.g. This country is in Europe. 59 million people live in this country. The flag is green, red and white. People eat pizza and pasta here! The capital city is Rome. People speak Italian. You can describe the countries or find audio on www.esolbooks.com.
   c) The students use the information on pages 192-194, to speak about the countries.
   d) Model the writing task by boarding the text about Italy, with the students' help – they then use the key words to write sentences about each country, referring back to the model if necessary.

5. ee/oo, pages 195-197
   Aim: phonics – ee and oo

   a) Board the Greek flag and clarify the sound-spelling link (ee - /i:/). See if the students can remember any 'ee' and 'oo' words learnt in previous units. Mime to elicit some of these, if necessary, e.g. food, spoon etc. Show the pictures from page 195 on the whiteboard for the students to name in pairs. Drill the words in open-class feedback.
   b) Reinforce the sound-spelling link through a minimal pairs drill where the students can shout out "double o" or "double e." Use the words from the pictures plus a few more, e.g. bedroom, sleep, pool, sheep, spoon, tree, moon, feet, bathroom, see, food, cheese, living room, three.
   c) The material features reading/writing practice. The students can read the words in the table aloud after copying them into the correct column.

6. abc, page 198
   Aim: phonics - initial consonant sounds

   Suggested words below:

   1. run
   2. ship
   3. when
   4. bin
   5. tiger
   6. kids
   7. people
   8. very
   9. chicken
   10. pool

7. Kahoot Quiz
   Aim: revision

   Finish the unit with a Kahoot quiz. Search 'TeacherGCC' (case specific) on Kahoot and look for the quiz for unit 10.

For a free Answer Key for every unit, visit www.esolbooks.com.

Unit 11: My friend

Speaking/reading/writing: describing a friend

Grammar and phonics: ‘s’ for third person verbs

1. My friend, pages 200-202
   Aims: speaking, reading and writing; grammar – third person s

   a) Show some pictures of a friend of yours and tell the students about them. Drill some phrases, e.g. “His name is ..., He is from..., He likes ....” after which the learners talk about a friend. Monitor to help, especially students who talk about a female as they’ll need to use her/she instead of his/he.
   b) For a pre-reading task, show pictures of Tom and his life and elicit information about him.
   c) The text and tasks provide the opportunity for reading aloud followed by reading comprehension.
   d) Focus on third person s by asking, “Do we say ‘Tom like gaming’ or ‘Tom likes gaming’?” Elicit the use of ‘s’ for he/she and drill some phrases from the text.
   e) Reinforce the use of ‘s’ with some open-class oral teacher-students interaction, for example:
      - The teacher says verbs, some first person and some third person and the students categorise them, e.g. Teacher: “have coffee every day”, Students: “I have coffee every day”, teacher: “lives in England”, students: “He lives in England” etc.
      - Try a substitution drill about Tom, nominating individuals, e.g. Teacher: “name-Tom”, student: “His name is Tom.”
      - Push the students a little more with a transformation drill, e.g. Teacher: “go”, student: “he goes.” Alternatively, try a question-and-answer drill, e.g. Teacher: “Where does he live?”, student: “He lives in England.”
   f) The tasks on pages 200-202 encourage practice of this language through reading/writing tasks.

g) Repeat the speaking task from earlier where the students talk about a friend but to keep it fresh the learners can change partners or run this as a class mingle so that everyone speaks to a different student.
h) The Workbook includes Dolch List practice of these words from the text: is, has, goes, he, she, his, her, lives, likes, watches. Plan a flash cards stage during this class, or the following day.

If you have time, create a text and tasks about a friend of yours instead of Tom as the students love finding about their teacher.

2. Hong, pages 203-206
Aims: speaking, reading and writing; grammar – third person s

a) Stage this in the same way as the lesson about 'Tom.' This text is similar but the students get some exposure to the pronouns her/she.
b) Remind the students about third person 's' and incorporate similar drills and speaking tasks to those above in the lesson about Tom. Tell the students to speak about a different friend to the one they spoke about in the previous lesson for some variety.
c) After a LSCWC stage to help them prepare, the students write about a friend. Stronger learners can extend texts and/or write about multiple friends.

3. Speak about a classmate, no material
Aims: speaking, reading and writing

a) Using the students in the room is a great way to personalise the language. In this lesson the students describe a classmate. Model the task through a student who is absent or your partner teacher, if you have one. Elicit information about him/her and drill some phrases.
b) Board key words about some students, e.g.

Ahmed
19
Sudan

Glasgow
Football and TV

The students use the key words to write texts about their classmates.

c) An alternative way to do this is to stage a mingle where the students interview each other and complete a questionnaire (monitor to help with spelling), e.g.

Name	Country	He/she likes...

The added bonus of this is that the students get to revise and practise spelling out their names and countries. They can use the table to write short texts.

A Mr Bean video is a fun way to give further practice of this language. Either use the LEA approach and collaboratively construct a text (e.g. Mr Bean goes to ...) or create your own worksheet.

4. 'Good or bad?', page 207
   Aims: reading, grammar revision

   a) Model the task and pair students to tick or cross the sentences depending on the grammar.
   b) In open-class feedback you could make this a competition, award points for correct answers and announce a winner at the end, who gets a huge round of applause from the class for winning!

5. ‘abc’, page 208
   Aim: phonics - initial consonant sounds

   Suggested words below:

1. so	6. not
2. chat	7. goes
3. have	8. see
4. make	9. she
5. like	10.time

6. Kahoot Quiz
   Aim: revision

   Finish the unit with a Kahoot quiz. Search ‘TeacherGCC’ (case specific) on Kahoot and look for the quiz for unit 11.

For a free Answer Key for every unit, visit www.esolbooks.com.

Unit 12: Jobs

Speaking/reading/writing: hopes and goals regarding future jobs; describing different jobs

Grammar: 's' for third person (revision)

Vocabulary: jobs

Phonics: er; 's' for third person (revision

Extra Material: Jobs vocabulary flash cards

1. Jobs, pages 210-211

   Aims: vocabulary – jobs; phonics – initial consonant sounds

   a) As a lead in, ask "What's my job?" and elicit other jobs. Ask "Which are good jobs?"
   b) Board the pictures from page 210 or distribute pictures on cards (in the Extra Materials section) for the students to work together to name. Clarify and drill the words in open-class feedback.
   c) The students use the initial consonant sounds to help them fill in the gaps on pages 210-211.

2. Jobs, pages 212-215
   Aims: Speaking, reading and writing

   a) Chat about jobs before introducing the texts, e.g. "Do you have a job?", "Did you have a job in your country?, "Do you want a job in future?"
   b) Show a picture of Mohammad on the board and see if the students can remember him. Show pictures of jobs mentioned in the text and tell the students about him and his future goals.
   c) The material enables practice of reading aloud and comprehension tasks.
   d) The controlled writing practice task on page 214 and the LSCWC task on page 215 help the students build up to the final freer writing task.
   e) Board a model of the type of text the students can write and encourage them to personalise their scripts.

f) The Workbook includes Dolch List practice of these words from the text: now, job, get, maybe, know, barber, student, good, more, work.

3. She is a teacher, pages 216-218
   Aims: speaking, reading and writing; grammar – 's' for third person (revision)

   a) Model the first speaking task through Kate. Encourage the learners to read the words aloud and to expand each word into a sentence, e.g. "Her name is Kate. She is a teacher." etc. The students describe the other people on this page in pairs.
   b) Page 217 features a slightly different reading task for the students so model the first 2 or 3 questions for them and monitor to help them read the task. Pairwork will make this more achievable.
   c) Remind the students about 'third person s', which was focused on in the previous unit, before they tackle the tasks on page 218. For example, ask "Do we say Kate like or likes her job"? Run some drills about the four workers, e.g. Teacher: "Kate", students: "Her name is Kate."
   d) Page 218 helps the students practise this language in a reading and writing task as well as providing a model for the next writing task in which they write about Nasser, Beth and Max.

4. My Teacher, page 219
   Aim: phonics – 'er'

   a) Drill the jobs which include 'er' so that the students can hear that these words rhyme.
   b) Write 'teacher' on the board and emphasise the sound and spelling link with the 'er' ending.
   c) Test the students orally by saying words including 'er' among others which don't. The students can respond with 'e-r' or 'no e-r.' Here are some words you could use for this: teacher, friend, working, student, builder, job, paper, cook, farmer, water, student, shop, barber, cleaner, computer, work.
   d) The students circle the letters 'er' in 'builder' and 'farmer' and then attempt the matching task.
   e) Finally, write the words on the board and nominate students to say the words.

5. abc, page 220
   Aim: phonics - initial consonant sounds

   Suggested words below:

1. now	6. job
2. taxi	7. run
3. water	8. home
4. make	9. cleaner
5. farmer	10. change

6. Kahoot Quiz
   Aim: revision

Finish the unit with a Kahoot quiz. Search 'TeacherGCC' (case specific) on Kahoot and look for the quiz for unit 12.

For a free Answer Key for every unit, visit www.esolbooks.com.

Unit 13: I'm sick

Speaking/reading/writing: what we do when we're sick;

Semi-authentic material: understanding a text from the dentist; understanding signs

Vocabulary: the body and face; illness and treatment

Phonics: ee and ea

Numeracy: important numbers in health and medicine

Extra Material: Signs flash cards

1. The body, pages 222-223

Aims: vocabulary – the body and face; phonics – initial consonant sounds

a) Point at your arm and ask, "What's that?" Elicit a few other body parts before displaying the pictures on page 222 on the board (with the arrows but no text). The students name as many of these words as possible.
b) The students use phonics to help them fill in the gaps on pages 222-223.

2. I'm sick, pages 224-226

Aims: Speaking, reading and writing

a) Ask the class, "What do you do when you sick?" Put them into small groups to discuss this. The students may mention medicine or, quite possibly, natural remedies.
b) Display pictures representing Andy and his preferred tools to combat ill health. Elicit these from the students.
c) The material enables practice of reading aloud and comprehension tasks on pages 224-226.
d) Board a model of the type of text the students can write and encourage them to personalise their scripts.

e) The Workbook includes Dolch List practice of these words from the text: take, tablets, happy, sleep, bed, tea, leg, sick, much, hand.

3. The Dentist, page 227

Aim: Understanding a semi-authentic text – a text message from the dentist

a) Show some images on the board to introduce the topic: appointments at the dentist. Ask the group a few questions, e.g. Do you have a dentist? Where? How often do you go? Do you like going to the dentist?
b) Ask how the students know about appointments. Do they receive text messages? Do they receive text messages for other appointments, e.g. GP, hospital, solicitor.
c) Tell the group that you are going to show them a text message which was sent to a patient. Ask them to predict the content, e.g. date and time of next appointment.
d) Show the group the text on the whiteboard and read it aloud. The group can then read aloud together.
e) The material includes a true or false task.
f) Finally, ask the students if they have received any texts like this one recently. If anyone is willing, they could show such a text message to their classmates while the teacher monitors to help.

4. Signs, pages 228-229
Aim: Understanding signs

a) Show some signs on the board to see which ones the students know. The matching task on page 228 provides more context for the signs.
b) See if the students can do the matching task without you reading the words aloud first. Encourage them to sound out the words while monitoring.
c) Finally, ask the students to look at signs 1-6 and shout out the number which matches your descriptions below:
   a. Don't smoke cigarettes here. (3)
   b. It's break time and I need to go to the toilet. (2)
   c. I need a drink, I'm going to the shop. I open the door because I can see from the sign that the shop is open. (5)
   d. It's 4 o'clock and the class is finished. I go downstairs and go to the door to leave the college. Above the door I see the exit sign. (4)

e. I go to the shop to buy some food but I can't go in because it's too late. The shop is closed. (6)
f. I'm sick. I want to buy some medicine. Where can I go? (1)

5. ee/ea, pages 230-232
Aim: phonics – ee and ea

a) Board the pictures of tea and a woman sleeping to clarify the /i:/ sound which both spellings have in common. See if the students can remember any 'ee' words learnt in previous units. Show the pictures from page 230 on the whiteboard for the students to name in pairs. Drill the words in open-class feedback.
b) Can the learners identify which words are spelt with 'ee' and which with 'ea'? They do the task on page 230 in pairs. The categorising task on page 231 helps them consolidate this.
c) Test them out orally in an open-class activity. Say the words and the learners respond with 'double e' or 'e-a.' For example, teacher: "sleep", students: "double e."
d) Finally, the students fill in the gaps on page 232.

6. I'm sick, page 233

Aims: Numeracy – understanding numbers in health and medicine

a) Use the pictures to set the context and make this into a class quiz. Display the pictures on the whiteboard (Power Point slides are on www.esolbooks.com) and ask the questions below. Put the students into groups of 3 and award points for correct answers.
   1. What's this? (thermometer) Where can you put this to check someone's temperature? (in the ear) What is a good temperature if you are NOT sick? (37 degrees)
   2. What is she taking? (pills / tablets)
   3. What's this? (medicine) What's this? (teaspoon)
   4. The man is badly hurt and needs an ambulance. Which number can I call? (999)
   5. The woman is reading a text from her GP about her next appointment. What information is in the text? (time and date of appointment, GP phone number)
b) The matching task should be achievable after the quiz but encourage the students to help each other and provide support yourself if necessary.

7. Numbers, page 234
   Aim: numeracy (revision)

   The teacher asks the students to identify the different numerical forms, e.g. "1, which number is a postcode?" Suggested questions below:

   a. A time?
   b. A postcode?
   c. A telephone number?
   d. A bus number?
   e. A date of birth?
   f. A flat, part of an address?
   g. A date of birth?
   h. A flat, part of an address?
   i. A year?
   j. A telephone number?

8. Kahoot Quiz
   Aim: revision

   Finish the unit with a Kahoot quiz. Search 'TeacherGCC' (case specific) on Kahoot and look for the quiz for unit 13.

For a free Answer Key for every unit, visit www.esolbooks.com.

Unit 14: Clothes

Speaking/reading/writing: describing what someone is wearing

Vocabulary: clothes; colours (revision)

Numeracy: prices, special offers, calculating change

Phonics: ing (revision)

Extra Material: Clothes vocabulary flash cards

1. Clothes, pages 236-237

   Aims: vocabulary – clothes; phonics – initial consonant sounds

   a) Point at some of your clothes and ask, "What's that?" Elicit and drill the phrase "I'm wearing" and put the students into pairs to name the clothes they are wearing.
   b) Show pictures of the clothes on page 236 on the board or distribute flash cards from the Extra Materials section. The learners name the items.
   c) The students use phonics to help them fill in the gaps on pages 236-237.

2. My clothes, pages 238-240

   Aims: Speaking, reading and writing

   a) Show the class a picture of Ali and ask "What is he wearing?"
   b) The material enables practice of reading aloud and comprehension tasks on pages 238-240.
   c) Board a model of the type of text the students can write and encourage them to personalise their scripts. Insist on them closing their coursebooks but allow them to have a quick look at the vocabulary of clothes if necessary to help with spelling. There may well be items of clothing that weren't clarified previously so write these on the board for the class.
   d) The Workbook includes Dolch List practice of these words from the text: red, wearing, blue, hat, dress, jacket, jeans, white, shirt, clothes.

3. He's wearing a hat, page 241
   Aim: Speaking, reading and writing

   a) Show the pictures of Bob, Sue and Sarah on the board for the students to describe.
   b) Ask a few of the questions on page 241 (with their books closed) for the students to shout out Bob, Sue, Sarah (or Sue AND Sarah!). The students repeat this but relying on the text on page 241.
   c) Using 'he's' or 'she's instead of a name, describe a student in class for the students to name. The students play this game in small groups.
   d) The students write about their classmates. If they have a photo of a friend/ relative they can also write about them ('In this photo he's wearing….').

4. How much? Pages 242-244
   Aims: Reading, speaking and listening – understanding phrases used in sales, buying clothes and giving change

   a) As a lead in, ask where the students buy their clothes and their favourite clothes.
   b) Model the next task by showing the picture of the woman wearing a pink jacket on page 242. Tell the students that she got the shoes and jacket at a very good price and she's very happy! Write the prices on the board and tell the students the deals '£5 off' and 'half price.' Can they tell you the new prices? Clarify the meaning of the two phrases.
   c) Encourage pair work to calculate the prices of the clothes on page 242. There are plenty of examples here which should help the learners understand the concept.
   d) Page 243 is revision of an area focused on in unit 6, which has the theme of 'food.' Use one of the items on page 242 as an example. For instance, "I got the sunglasses for £10 and I give £20. Any change?" Display page 243 on the board to model the next task. Read question 1 aloud and elicit the answer.
   e) The audio for the listening task can be found on www.esolbooks.com. Read the questions aloud first of all. If you think your students will struggle to read and listen at the same time, then this could be set orally.
   f) Play the audio again and pause it to elicit some useful phrases, e.g.
      - Excuse me, can you help me please?
      - I'm looking for a white t-shirt.
      - Do you have a bigger one?
      - How much is it?

- Can I pay by card?

g) Model a role play by choosing a stronger student to play the role of customer. The students can then perform this in pairs. It's good fun to have everyone stand up for this and divide the class into shop assistants and customers. The customers mingle and look for a shop assistant. After a while they can reverse roles. Let them invent the items they are looking for and the prices. This usually results in some improvised fun!

5. abc, page 245
   Aim: phonics - initial consonant sounds

   Suggested words below:

   1. very
   2. China
   3. date
   4. brown
   5. take
   6. nice
   7. price
   8. sleep
   9. shoes
   10. give

6. Kahoot Quiz
   Aim: revision

   Finish the unit with a Kahoot quiz. Search 'TeacherGCC' (case specific) on Kahoot and look for the quiz for unit 14.

For a free Answer Key for every unit, visit www.esolbooks.com.

Extra Materials

Many of the materials on the following pages are intended to be photocopied and cut out for students to use.

Activity	Unit	Student's Book Page(s)	Activity
1	1	19-29	Classroom objects vocabulary flashcards
2	1	27-30	Numbers 0-10 flash cards (numeric form)
3	1	27-30	Numbers 0-10 bingo (numeric form)
4	2	36-37	Free time vocabulary flash cards
5	2	43-45	Numbers 10-20 flash cards (numeric form)
6	2	43-45	Numbers 10-20 bingo (numeric form)
7	3	48-49	Routines vocabulary flash cards
8	3	54-56	Time-telling flash cards
9	3	61	Days of the week flash cards
10	4	70-71	Vehicles flash cards
11	4	77-79	Numbers 0-100 bingo (numeric form)
12	5	84-85	Places in a town/city vocabulary flash cards
13	5	97-101	Years flash cards
14	6	108-109	Food vocabulary flash cards
15	6	118-121	Prices flash cards
16	7	130-131	Weather vocabulary flash cards
17	7	132-134	Months of the year vocabulary flash cards
18	8	146-147	Christmas vocabulary flash cards

19	9	172-173	Furniture and household appliances vocabulary flash cards
20	9	174-175	Numbers 1-10 flash cards (written form)
21	9	174-175	Numbers 1-10 bingo (written form)
22	10	190-191	Colours vocabulary flash cards
23	12	210-211	Jobs vocabulary flash cards
24	13	229	Signs flash cards
25	14	236-237	Clothes vocabulary flash cards

1. Classroom objects vocabulary flash cards

Unit 1, pages 19-20

Instructions

a. Before the class, print a set of flash cards to give each pair of students. Cut them out ready for the class. These cards could be used when you first clarify the vocabulary or the next day as revision.
b. Give the students the picture cards first without the words. They work in pairs to name the words. Monitor to help with the vocabulary and help the class with pronunciation. Use the board to check the answers with the group. Go to www.esolbooks.com for free Power Point slides.
c. You could consolidate this by having the students spread the cards out in front of them and shouting out a word/phrase for the students. They respond by holding up the picture and shouting out the number, e.g. "Teacher: rubber!", students: "number 6!" Also, instruct the students to test each other in pairs, i.e. a student takes a card and asks their partner, "What's that?"
d. The students work in pairs to match the pictures to the words. Monitor to help, encouraging the learners to use the initial consonant and then check each group has done this correctly. This is enough in terms of checking answers as the gap-fill task on page 19 clarifies the spelling.
e. Use the board to show the words and elicit the initial consonant sounds and any interesting phonics, e.g. digraphs like the 'ch' in 'teacher', the 'er' rime in 'rubber.' Go to www.esolbooks.com for free Power Point slides.
f. The students remove the pictures so that they only have the words in front of them. Say the words (e.g. Teacher: "notebook!") and the first student to hold up the word is awarded a point for their team. Finally, the students read the words on the cards aloud, in pairs.
g. If you used these cards to clarify the vocabulary, then the class can move to the initial consonant gap-fill on page 19.

1. 	2. 	3. 
4. 	5. 	6. 
students	**college**	**teacher**
notebook	**pencil**	**rubber**

2. Numbers 0-10 flash cards (numeric form)

Unit 1, pages 27-30

Instructions

a. Before the class, print a set of flash cards to give each pair of students. Cut them out ready for the class.
b. Split the group into pairs and give them the numbers to reorder. Monitor and check that each pair has done this correctly and/or use the board to check the answers with the group. Go to www.esolbooks.com for free Power Point slides.
c. Instruct them to spread the numbers out in front of them. Say the numbers (e.g. Teacher: "nine!") and the first student to hold up the number is awarded a point for their team.
d. Finally, the learners test each other in pairs, i.e. a student takes a card and asks their partner, "What's that?" Alternatively, you could do this as a class mingle.

0	6
1	7
2	8
3	9
4	10
5	

3. Numbers 0-10 bingo (numeric form)

Unit 1, pages 27-30

Instructions

a. Before the class, print a set of bingo cards to give each pair of students. Cut them out ready for the class.
b. Split the group into pairs and give them their bingo card. Instruct them to read the numbers aloud.
c. Tell the class the objective of bingo: cross off all your numbers and shout out "bingo!"
d. Read numbers aloud for the students to cross numbers off. Make a note of the numbers so you can check if the winners have listened accurately!

1	3
6	9

0	1
5	8

3	5
7	10

2	4
6	8

1	5
6	9

0	1
4	10

1	3
5	7

2	5
8	9

0	4
6	10

Record of numbers called out:

GAME 1: 0 1 2 3 4 5 6 7 8 9 10 **GAME 3:** 0 1 2 3 4 5 6 7 8 9 10

GAME 2: 0 1 2 3 4 5 6 7 8 9 10 **GAME 4:** 0 1 2 3 4 5 6 7 8 9 10

4. Free time vocabulary flash cards

Unit 2, pages 36-37

Instructions

a. Before the class, print a set of flash cards to give each pair of students. Cut them out ready for the class. These cards could be used when you first clarify the vocabulary or the next day as revision.

b. Give the students the picture cards first without the words. They work in pairs to name the words. Use the board to check the answers with the group. Go to www.esolbooks.com for free Power Point slides. You could consolidate this by having the students spread the cards out in front of them and shouting out a word/phrase for the students. They respond by holding up the picture and shouting out the number, e.g. "Teacher: I watch TV every day", students: "number 3!" Also, instruct the students to test each other in pairs, i.e. a student takes a card and asks their partner, "What's that?"

c. The students work in pairs to match the pictures to the words. Monitor to help, encouraging the learners to use the initial consonant and then check each group has done this correctly. This is enough in terms of checking answers as the gap-fill task on page 36 clarifies the spelling.

d. Use the board to show the words and elicit the initial consonant sounds, silent letters, any interesting phonics, e.g. digraphs like sh/ch, rimes such as the 'ing' in 'swimming' or the 'sh' in 'shopping.' Go to www.esolbooks.com for free Power Point slides.

e. The students remove the pictures so that they only have the words in front of them. Say the words (e.g. Teacher: "swimming!") and the first student to hold up the word is awarded a point for their team. Finally, the students read the words on the cards aloud, in pairs.

f. If you used these cards to clarify the vocabulary, then the class can move to the initial consonant gap-fill on page 36.

1. 	2. 	3. 
4. 	5. 	6. 
7. 	8. 	9. 
shopping	**swimming**	**watch TV**
music	**friends**	**gaming**
reading	**football**	**the gym**

5. Numbers 10-20 flash cards (numeric form)

Unit 2, pages 43-45

Instructions

a. Before the class, print a set of flash cards to give each pair of students. Cut them out ready for the class.
b. Split the group into pairs and give them the numbers to reorder. Monitor and check that each pair has done this correctly.
c. Instruct them to spread the numbers out in front of them. Say the numbers (e.g. Teacher: "15!") and the first student to hold up the number is awarded a point for their team.
d. Finally, the learners test each other in pairs, i.e. a student takes a card and asks their partner, "What's that?" Alternatively, you could do this as a class mingle.

10	16
11	17
12	18
13	19
14	20
15	

6. Numbers 0-20 bingo (numeric form)

Unit 2, pages 43-45

Instructions

a. Before the class, print a set of bingo cards to give each pair of students. Cut them out ready for the class.
b. Split the group into pairs and give them their bingo card. Instruct them to read the numbers aloud.
c. Tell the class the objective of bingo: cross off all your numbers and shout out "bingo!"
d. Read numbers aloud for the students to cross numbers off. Make a note of the numbers so you can check if the winners have listened accurately!

1	4	5
9	11	12
14	16	20

0	1	6
10	13	15
15	18	19

1	2	7
9	10	12
15	17	20

3	4	6
8	11	12
14	16	20

1	3	7
8	10	13
14	17	19

0	2	4
7	11	12
14	16	18

0	3	5
8	11	14
16	17	20

1	2	5
6	9	13
15	18	20

1	6	8
9	13	15
16	17	19

2	3	9
11	13	14
15	17	20

0	5	9
11	14	15
16	17	19

2	6	7
10	11	13
14	15	20

Record of numbers called out:

GAME 1: 0 1 2 3 4 5 6 7 8 9 10 11 12 13 14 15 16 17 18 19 20

GAME 2: 0 1 2 3 4 5 6 7 8 9 10 11 12 13 14 15 16 17 18 19 20

GAME 3: 0 1 2 3 4 5 6 7 8 9 10 11 12 13 14 15 16 17 18 19 20

GAME 4: 0 1 2 3 4 5 6 7 8 9 10 11 12 13 14 15 16 17 18 19 20

7. Routines vocabulary flash cards

Unit 3, pages 48-49

Instructions

a. Before the class, print a set of flash cards to give each pair of students. Cut them out ready for the class. These cards could be used when you first clarify the vocabulary or the next day as revision.
b. Give the students the picture cards first without the words. They work in pairs to name the words. Use the board to check the answers with the group. Go to www.esolbooks.com for free Power Point slides. You could consolidate this by having the students spread the cards out in front of them and shouting out a word/phrase for the students. They respond by holding up the picture and shouting out the number, e.g. "Teacher: I go to bed at 10 o'clock every day", students: "number 9!" Also, instruct the students to test each other in pairs, i.e. a student takes a card and asks their partner, "What's that?"
c. The students work in pairs to match the pictures to the words. Monitor to help, encouraging the learners to use the initial consonant and then check each group has done this correctly. This is enough in terms of checking answers as the gap-fill task on page 48 clarifies the spelling.
d. Use the board to show the words and elicit the initial consonant sounds, silent letters, any interesting phonics, e.g. the long vowel sound for the 'ee' in 'teeth', the silent e in 'have.' Go to www.esolbooks.com for free Power Point slides.
e. The students remove the pictures so that they only have the words in front of them. Say the words (e.g. Teacher: "go to college!") and the first student to hold up the word is awarded a point for their team. Finally, the students read the words on the cards aloud, in pairs.
f. If you used these cards to clarify the vocabulary, then the class can move to the initial consonant gap-fill on page 48.

1. 	2. 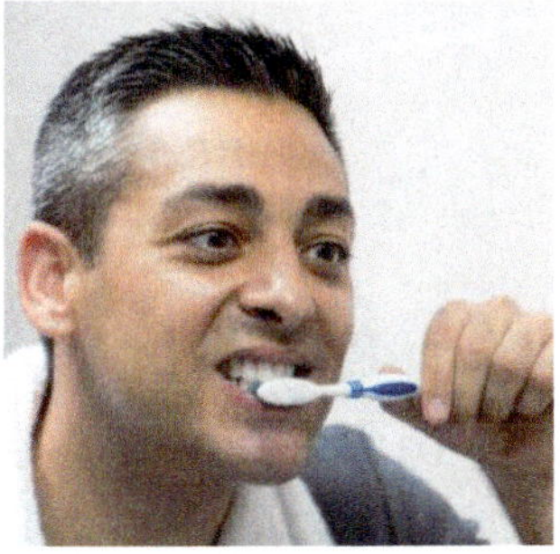	3. 
4. 	5. 	6. 
7. 	8. 	9. 
have dinner	**brush my teeth**	**have a shower**
have breakfast	**go to college**	**clean my flat**
get up	**watch TV**	**go to bed**

8. Time-telling flash cards

Unit 3, pages 54-56

Instructions

a. Before the class, print a set of flash cards to give each pair of students. Cut them out ready for the class. Use these cards for extra practise after clarifying how to tell the time.

b. As a warm-up, give out the cards and have the students spread them out on their desks. Say a time and the students can pick up the correct card and the number. For example, teacher: "It's 4 o'clock", students: "Number 10."

c. Set the main task to use these cards for. Remind the class of the question "What's the time?" Model the task: a student takes a card and asks their partner the question. Monitor to check they are answering correctly.

d. Fast finishers can mix the cards up and repeat the task.

e. You could show some of the clock faces on the board and nominate individuals to answer. Go to www.esolbooks.com for free Power Point slides.

f. This could also be done as a mingle with one set of cards. For this, give each student one card, everyone stands up and finds another student. They repeat the task from step c. They then swap cards and find a new partner.

1.

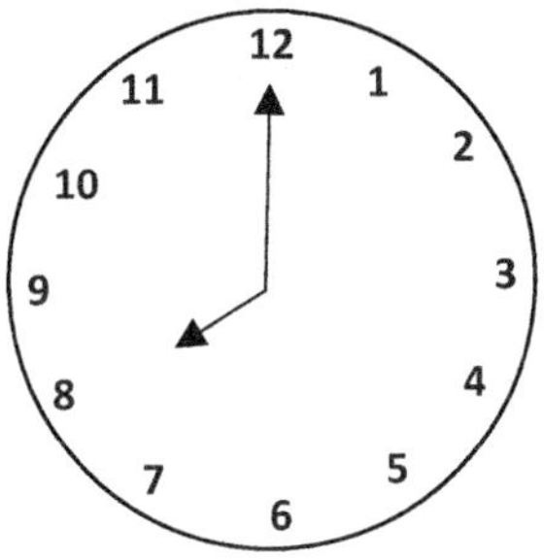

2.

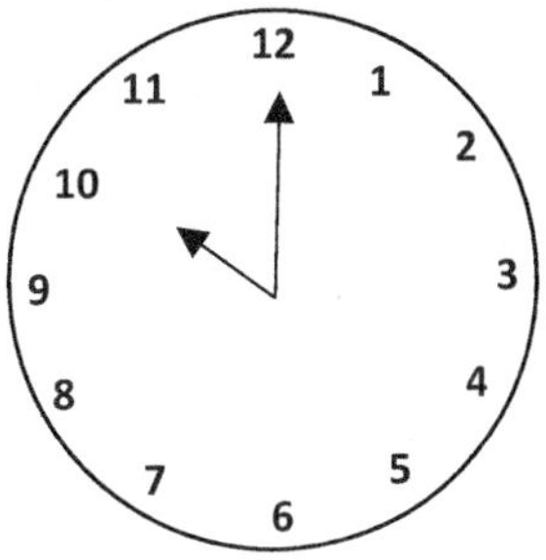

3.

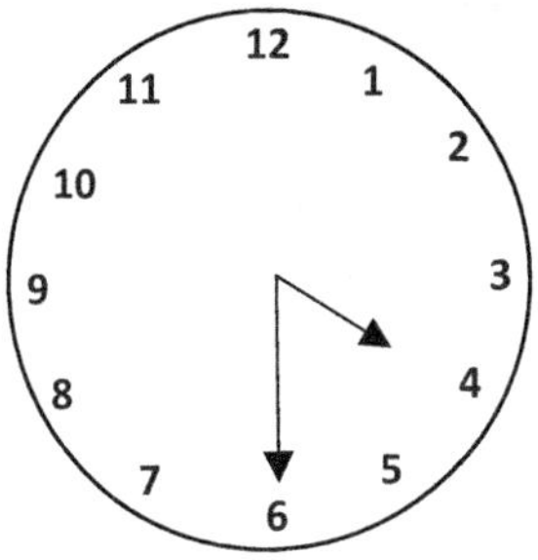

4.

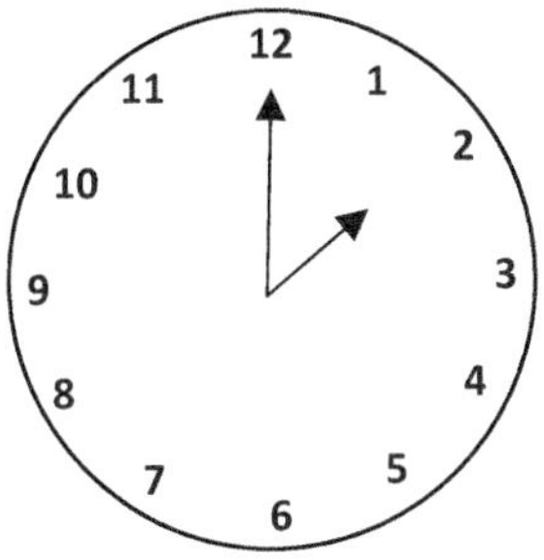

5.

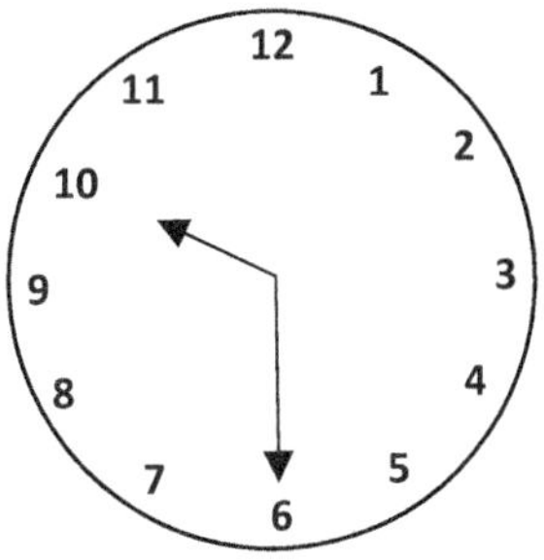

6.

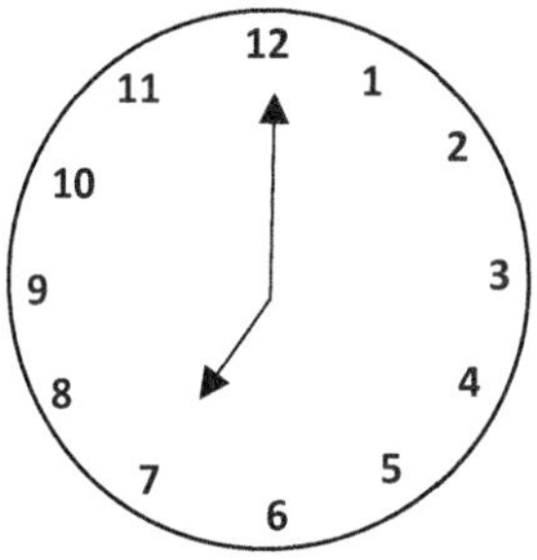

7.

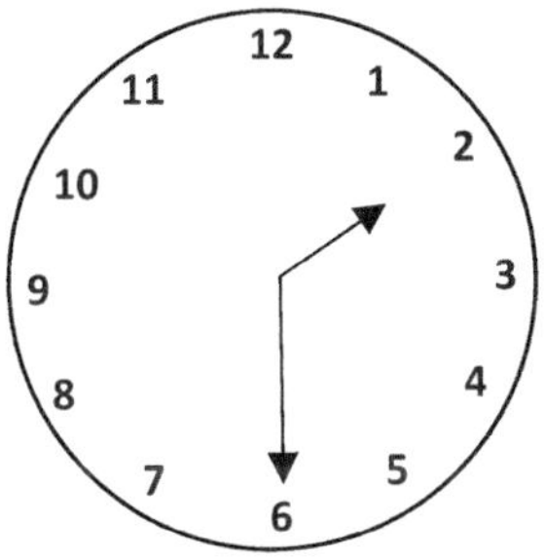

8.

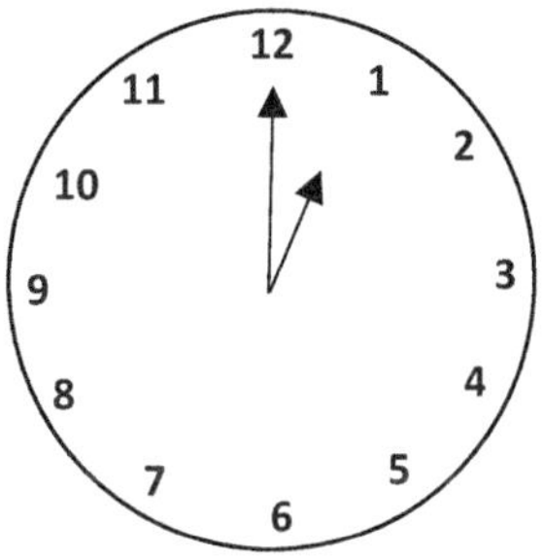

9.

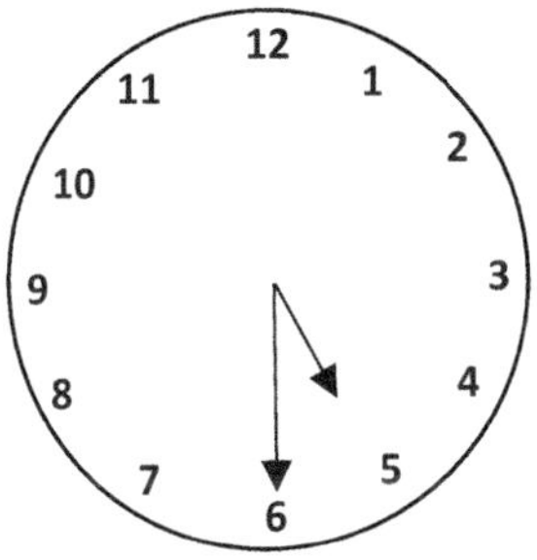

10.

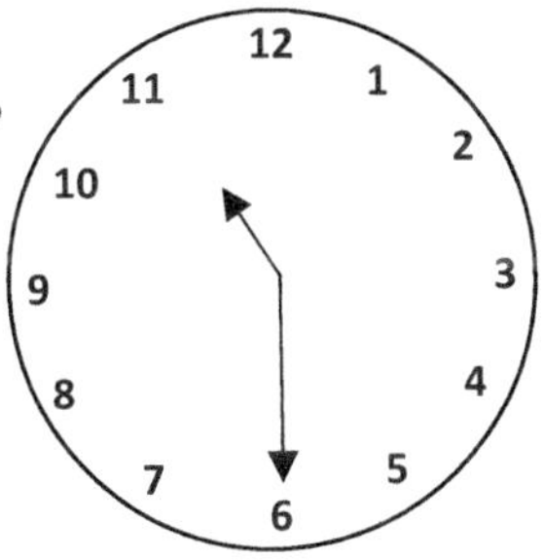

11.

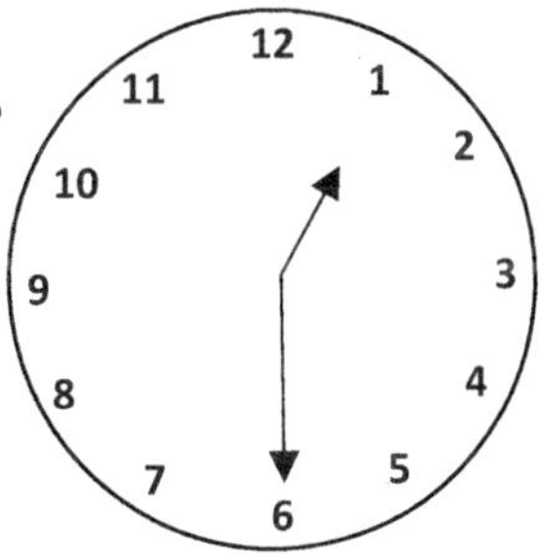

12.

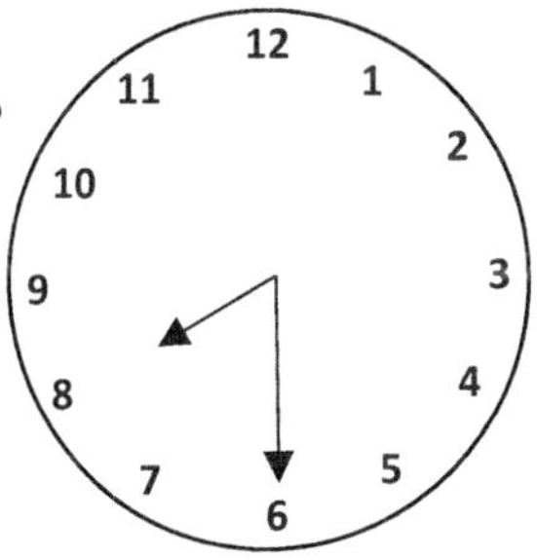

13.

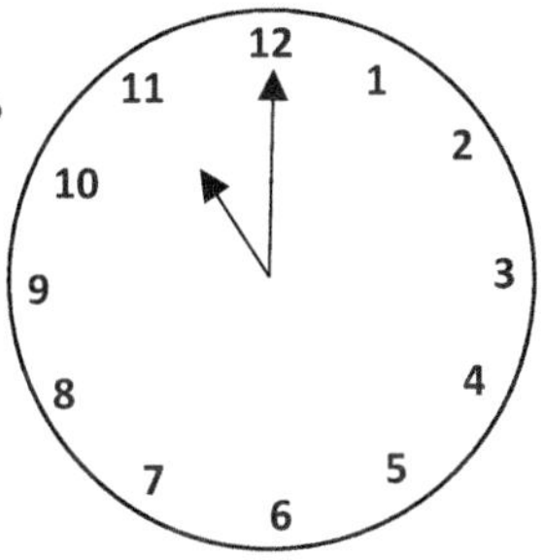

14.

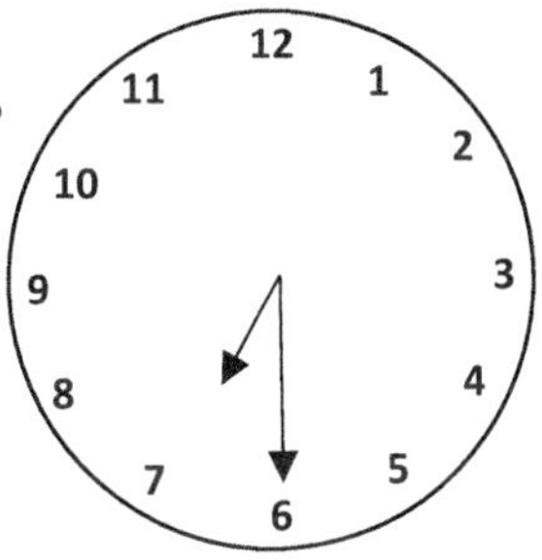

15.

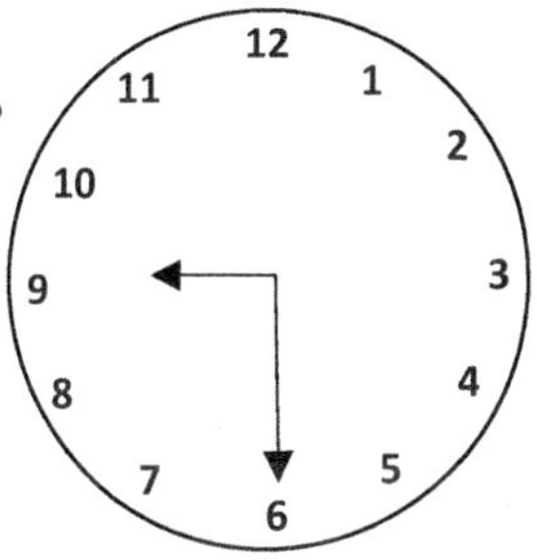

9. Days of the week vocabulary flash cards

Unit 3, page 61

Instructions

a. Before the class, print a set of flash cards, constituting the 7 days of the week, to give each pair of students. Cut them out ready for the class. These cards could be used when you first clarify the vocabulary or the next day as revision.

b. Split the group into pairs and give them the days to reorder. Monitor to help, encouraging the learners to use the initial consonant and then check each group has done this correctly. This is enough in terms of checking answers as the gap-fill task on page 61 clarifies the spelling.

c. Use the board to show the words and elicit the initial consonant sounds, silent letters, any interesting phonics, e.g. the 'ay' rime in every word. It's also worth eliciting that each of these begins with a capital letter. Go to www.esolbooks.com for free Power Point slides.

d. Instruct them to spread the cards out in front of them. Say a day (e.g. Teacher: "Friday!") and the first student to hold up the card is awarded a point for their team. You can increase the difficulty here by displaying the days randomly on the board and asking, "Which day is that?"

e. The learners can test each other in pairs, i.e. a student takes a card and asks their partner, "What's that?" Alternatively, you could do this as a class mingle.

f. If you used these cards before the material in the Student's Book, then you can move onto the tasks on page 61.

Monday	**Monday**
Tuesday	**Tuesday**
Wednesday	**Wednesday**
Thursday	**Thursday**
Friday	**Friday**
Saturday	**Saturday**
Sunday	**Sunday**

10. Vehicles vocabulary flash cards

Unit 4, pages 70-71

Instructions

a. Before the class, print a set of flash cards to give each pair of students. Cut them out ready for the class. These cards could be used when you first clarify the vocabulary or the next day as revision.
b. Give the students the picture cards first without the words. They work in pairs to name the words. Use the board to check the answers with the group. Go to www.esolbooks.com for free Power Point slides. You could consolidate this by having the students spread the cards out in front of them and shouting out a word/phrase for the students. They respond by holding up the picture and shouting out the number, e.g. Teacher: "taxi", students: "number 6!" If they find this easy, ask instead, "What's number 9?", students: "lorry!" Also, instruct the students to test each other in pairs, i.e. a student takes a card and asks their partner, "What's that?"
c. The students work in pairs to match the pictures to the words. Monitor to help, encouraging the learners to use the initial consonant and then check each group has done this correctly. This is enough in terms of checking answers as the gap-fill task on page 70 clarifies the vocabulary and spelling also.
d. Use the board to show the words and elicit the initial consonant sounds, silent letters, any interesting phonics, e.g. the 'sh' in 'ship', the final /i:/ sound of the 'y' in 'lorry', the /ks/ sound of the 'x' in 'taxi.' Go to www.esolbooks.com for free Power Point slides.
e. The students remove the pictures so that they only have the words in front of them. Say the words (e.g. Teacher: "ship!") and the first student to hold up the word is awarded a point for their team. Finally, the students read the words on the cards aloud, in pairs.
f. If you used these cards to clarify the vocabulary, then the class can move to the initial consonant gap-fill on page 70.

1. 	2. 	3. 
4. 	5. 	6. 
7. 	8. 	9. 
bus	**bike**	**boat**
ship	**train**	**taxi**
van	**plane**	**lorry**

11. Numbers 0-100 bingo (numeric form)

Unit 4, pages 77-79

Instructions

a. Before the class, print a set of bingo cards to give each pair of students. Cut them out ready for the class.
b. Split the group into pairs and give them their bingo card. Instruct them to read the numbers aloud.
c. Tell the class the objective of bingo: cross off all your numbers and shout out "bingo!"
d. Read numbers aloud for the students to cross numbers off. Make a note of the numbers so you can check if the winners have listened accurately!

10	23	32
48	53	69
75	89	100

8	22	39
40	52	69
76	80	99

7	23	30
44	57	60
78	83	95

19	21	33
42	59	63
71	87	92

1	29	32
45	52	67
77	84	90

12	27	38
42	58	61
79	81	92

15	24	39
49	51	67
76	81	92

17	22	34
40	53	62
73	87	96

11	20	32
42	58	63
70	82	94

13	28	37
48	52	69
73	80	100

9	28	30
41	55	69
71	89	92

14	25	37
45	59	60
77	83	99

Record of numbers called out:

0 1 2 3 4 5 6 7 8 9 10 11 12 13 14 15 16 17 18 19 20 21 22
23 24 25 26 27 28 29 30 31 32 33 34 35 36 37 38 39 40 41 42
43 44 45 46 47 48 49 50 51 52 53 54 55 56 57 58 59 60 61 62
63 64 65 66 67 68 69 70 71 72 73 74 75 76 77 78 79 80 81 82
83 84 85 86 87 88 89 90 91 92 93 94 95 96 97 98 99 100

12. Places in a town/city vocabulary flash cards

Unit 5, pages 84-85

Instructions

a. Before the class, print a set of flash cards to give each pair of students. Cut them out ready for the class. These cards could be used when you first clarify the vocabulary or the next day as revision.

b. Give the students the picture cards first without the words. They work in pairs to name the words. Use the board to check the answers with the group. Go to www.esolbooks.com for free Power Point slides. You could consolidate this by having the students spread the cards out in front of them and shouting out a word/phrase for the students. They respond by holding up the picture and shouting out the number, e.g. Teacher: "shops!", students: "number 6!" If they find this easy, ask instead, "What's number 2?", students: "the park!" Also, instruct the students to test each other in pairs, i.e. a student takes a card and asks their partner, "What's that?"

c. The students work in pairs to match the pictures to the words. Monitor to help, encouraging the learners to use the initial consonant and then check each group has done this correctly. This is enough in terms of checking answers as the gap-fill task on page 84 clarifies the spelling.

d. Use the board to show the words and elicit the initial consonant sounds and any interesting phonics, e.g. you could contrast the /s/ sound in 'cinema' and the /k/ sound in 'college.' Go to www.esolbooks.com for free Power Point slides.

e. The students remove the pictures so that they only have the words in front of them. Say the words (e.g. Teacher: "the park!") and the first student to hold up the word is awarded a point for their team. Finally, the students read the words on the cards aloud, in pairs.

f. If you used these cards to clarify the vocabulary, then the class can move to the initial consonant gap-fill on page 84.

1. 	2. 	3. 
4. 	5. 	6. 
7. 	8. 	9. 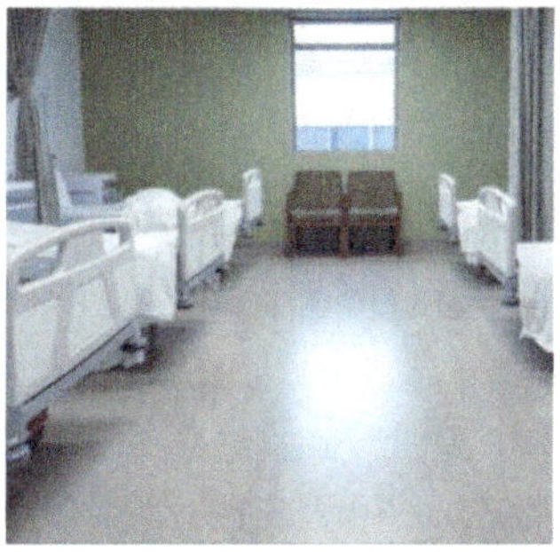
college	**park**	**cafe**
bank	**library**	**shops**
the gym	**cinema**	**hospital**

13. Years flash cards

Unit 5, pages 97-101

Instructions

a. Before the class, print a set of flash cards to give each pair of students. Cut them out ready for the class. Use these cards for extra practise after clarifying how to say prices.

b. As a warm-up, give out the cards and have the students spread them out on their desks. Say a year and the students can pick up the correct card.

c. For the next task, the pairs put the years in chronological order.

d. Set the main task to use these cards for. Model the task: a student takes a card and says the year. Monitor to check they are answering correctly.

e. Fast finishers can mix the cards up and repeat the task.

f. You could show some of the years on the board and nominate individuals to answer. Go to www.esolbooks.com for free Power Point slides.

g. This could also be done as a mingle with one set of cards. For this, give each student one card, everyone stands up and finds another student. They repeat the task from step d. They then swap cards and find a new partner.

1920	1990	2018
1955	1995	2020
1970	2001	2021
1982	2004	2022
1987	2008	2023
1989	2012	2024

14. Food vocabulary flash cards

Unit 6, pages 108-109

Instructions

a. Before the class, print a set of flash cards to give each pair of students. Cut them out ready for the class. These cards could be used when you first clarify the vocabulary or the next day as revision.

b. Give the students the picture cards first without the words. They work in pairs to name the words. Use the board to check the answers with the group. Go to www.esolbooks.com for free Power Point slides. You could consolidate this by having the students spread the cards out in front of them and shouting out a word/phrase for the students. They respond by holding up the picture and shouting out the number, e.g. Teacher: "I like chocolate!", students: "number 6!" If they find this easy, ask instead, "What's number 2?", students: "tomatoes!" Also, instruct the students to test each other in pairs, i.e. a student takes a card and asks their partner, "What's that?"

c. The students work in pairs to match the pictures to the words. Monitor to help, encouraging the learners to use the initial consonant and check each group has done this correctly. This is enough in terms of checking answers as the gap-fill task on page 108 clarifies the spelling.

d. Use the board to show the words and elicit the initial consonant sounds and any interesting phonics, e.g. the use of letter 's' (sound /s/) for plural countable nouns. Go to www.esolbooks.com for free Power Point slides.

e. The students remove the pictures so that they only have the words in front of them. Say the words (e.g. Teacher: "rice!") and the first student to hold up the word is awarded a point for their team. Finally, the students read the words on the cards aloud, in pairs.

f. If you used these cards to clarify the vocabulary, then the class can move to the initial consonant gap-fill on page 108.

1. 	2. 	3. 
4. 	5. 	6. 
7. 	8. 	9. 

tea	**tomatoes**	**rice**
bread	**chocolate**	**carrots**
orange juice	**fish**	**chicken**

15. Prices flash cards

Unit 6, pages 118-121

Instructions

a. Before the class, print a set of flash cards to give each pair of students. Cut them out ready for the class. Use these cards for extra practise after clarifying how to say prices.

b. As a warm-up, give out the cards and have the students spread them out on their desks. Say a price and the students can pick up the correct card.

c. Set the main task to use these cards for. Remind the class of the question "How much is it?" Model the task: a student takes a card and asks their partner the question. Monitor to check they are answering correctly.

d. Fast finishers can mix the cards up and repeat the task.

e. You could show some of the prices on the board and nominate individuals to answer. Go to www.esolbooks.com for free Power Point slides.

f. This could also be done as a mingle with one set of cards. For this, give each student one card, everyone stands up and finds another student. They repeat the task from step c. They then swap cards and find a new partner.

1p	85p	£20
2p	99p	£27
5p	£1	£50
10p	£1.25	£100
20p	£5	£200
50p	£10.50	£500

16. Weather vocabulary flash cards

Unit 7, pages 130-131

Instructions

a. Before the class, print a set of flash cards to give each pair of students. Cut them out ready for the class. These cards could be used when you first clarify the vocabulary or the next day as revision.

b. Give the students the picture cards first without the words. They work in pairs to name the words. Clarify the vocabulary and help the class with pronunciation. You could consolidate this through shouting out a word/phrase for the students. They respond by holding up the picture and shouting out the number, e.g. Teacher: "It's raining!", students: "number 2!" If they find this easy, ask instead, "Number 4, how's the weather?", students: "It's snowing!" Also, instruct the students to test each other in pairs, i.e. a student takes a card and asks their partner, "How's the weather?"

c. The students work in pairs to match the pictures to the words. Monitor to help, encouraging the learners to use the initial consonant and check each group has done this correctly. This is enough in terms of checking answers as the gap-fill task on page 130 clarifies the spelling.

d. Use the board to show the words and elicit the initial consonant sounds and any interesting phonics, e.g. the 'ing' in 'raining' and the /i:/ sound for the final 'y' in 'windy' and in 'cloudy.' Go to www.esolbooks.com for free Power Point slides.

e. The students remove the pictures so that they only have the words in front of them. Say the words (e.g. Teacher: "It's windy!") and the first student to hold up the word is awarded a point for their team. Finally, the students read the words on the cards aloud, in pairs.

f. If you used these cards to clarify the vocabulary, then the class can move to the initial consonant gap-fill on page 130.

1. 

2. 

3. 

4. 

5. 

6. 

cold	**hot**
raining	**snowing**
cloudy	**windy**

17. Months of the year flash cards

Unit 7, pages 132-134

Instructions

a. Before the class, print a set of flash cards to give each pair of students. Cut them out ready for the class. Clarify and practise this language orally before introducing the written words, either through these cards or through the material in the Student's Book, in which case these cards could be used the next day as revision.

b. Split the group into pairs and give them the months to reorder. Monitor to help, encouraging the learners to use the initial consonant and check each group has done this correctly. This is enough in terms of checking answers as the gap-fill task on page 132 clarifies the spelling.

c. Use the board to show the words and elicit the initial consonant sounds, silent letters, any interesting phonics, e.g. the 'ember' rime in many of the months. It's also worth eliciting that each of these begins with a capital letter. Go to www.esolbooks.com for free Power Point slides.

d. Instruct them to spread the cards out in front of them. Say a month (e.g. Teacher: "May!") and the first student to hold up the card is awarded a point for their team. You can increase the difficulty here by displaying the days randomly on the board and asking "Which month is that?"

e. The learners can test each other in pairs, i.e. a student takes a card and asks their partner, "What's that?" Alternatively, you could do this as a class mingle.

f. If you used these cards before the material in the Student's Book, then you can move onto the tasks on page 132.

January	July
February	August
March	September
April	October
May	November
June	December

18. Christmas vocabulary flash cards

Unit 8, pages 146-147

Instructions

a. Before the class, print a set of flash cards to give each pair of students. Cut them out ready for the class. These cards could be used when you first clarify the vocabulary or the next day as revision.
b. Give the students the picture cards first without the words. They work in pairs to name the words. Use the board to check the answers with the group. Go to www.esolbooks.com for free Power Point slides. You could consolidate this through shouting out a word/phrase for the students. They respond by holding up the picture and shouting out the number, e.g. Teacher: "Father Christmas!", students: "number 4!" If they find this easy, ask instead, "What's number 2?", students: "Christmas dinner!" Also, instruct the students to test each other in pairs, i.e. a student takes a card and asks their partner, "What's that?"
c. The students work in pairs to match the pictures to the words. Monitor to help, encouraging the learners to use the initial consonant and then check each group has done this correctly. This is enough in terms of checking answers as the gap-fill task on page 146 clarifies the vocabulary and spelling also.
d. Use the board to show the words and elicit the initial consonant sounds and any interesting phonics, e.g. the /OI/ sound for 'oy' in 'toy' and the /k/ sound for 'ch' in 'Christmas' (it's worth pointing out that this is much less common than the usual sound for 'ch' focused on in unit 1. Go to www.esolbooks.com for free Power Point slides.
e. The students remove the pictures so that they only have the words in front of them. Say the words (e.g. Teacher: "toys!") and the first student to hold up the word is awarded a point for their team. Finally, the students read the words on the cards aloud, in pairs.
f. If you used these cards to clarify the vocabulary, then the class can move to the initial consonant gap-fill on page 146.

1. 	2. 	3. 
4. 	5. 	6. 

Christmas tree	Christmas dinner
Father Christmas	Christmas cards
toys	gifts

19. Furniture and household appliances vocabulary flash cards

Unit 9, pages 172-173

Instructions

a. Before the class, print a set of flash cards to give each pair of students. Cut them out ready for the class. These cards could be used when you first clarify the vocabulary or the next day as revision.
b. Give the students the picture cards first without the words. They work in pairs to name the words. Use the board to check the answers with the group. Go to www.esolbooks.com for free Power Point slides. You could consolidate this through shouting out a word/phrase for the students. They respond by holding up the picture and shouting out the number, e.g. Teacher: "washing machine!", students: "number 1!" If they find this easy, ask instead, "What's number 6?", students: "cooker!" Also, instruct the students to test each other in pairs, i.e. a student takes a card and asks their partner, "What's that?"
c. The students work in pairs to match the pictures to the words. Monitor to help, encouraging the learners to use the initial consonant and then check each group has done this correctly. This is enough in terms of checking answers as the gap-fill task on page 172 clarifies the spelling.
d. Use the board to show the words and elicit the initial consonant sounds and any interesting phonics, e.g. the double appearance of 'sh' in 'dishwasher.' Go to www.esolbooks.com for free Power Point slides.
e. The students remove the pictures so that they only have the words in front of them. Say the words (e.g. Teacher: "table!") and the first student to hold up the word is awarded a point for their team. Finally, the students read the words on the cards aloud, in pairs.
f. If you used these cards to clarify the vocabulary, then the class can move to the initial consonant gap-fill on page 172.

1. 

2. 

3. 

4. 

5. 

6. 

7. 

8. 

9. 

washing machine	microwave	dishwasher
chair	cooker	sofa
bed	table	fridge

20. Numbers 1-10 flash cards (written form)

Unit 9, pages 174-175

Instructions

a. Before the class, print a set of flash cards to give each pair of students. Cut them out ready for the class.
b. Split the group into pairs and give them the numbers to reorder. Monitor and check that each pair has done this correctly. This is enough in terms of checking answers as the gap-fill task on page 174 clarifies the spelling.
c. Instruct them to spread the numbers out in front of them. Say the numbers (e.g. Teacher: "nine!") and the first student to hold up the card is awarded a point for their team.
d. Finally, the learners test each other in pairs, i.e. a student takes a card and asks their partner, "What's that?" Alternatively, you could do this as a class mingle.
e. Move onto the gap-fill on page 174.

one	six
two	seven
three	eight
four	nine
five	ten

21. Numbers 0-10 bingo (written form)

Unit 9, pages 174-175

Instructions

a. Before the class, print a set of bingo cards to give each pair of students. Cut them out ready for the class.
b. Split the group into pairs and give them their bingo card. Instruct them to read the numbers aloud.
c. Tell the class the objective of bingo: cross off all your numbers and shout out "bingo!"
d. Read numbers aloud for the students to cross numbers off. Make a note of the numbers so you can check if the winners have listened accurately!

one	three
six	nine

two	four
five	eight

three	five
seven	ten

two	four
six	nine

one	five
six	ten

two	five
seven	ten

one	three
five	nine

two	five
six	ten

one	two
seven	ten

Record of numbers called out:

GAME 1: 0 1 2 3 4 5 6 7 8 9 10 **GAME 3:** 0 1 2 3 4 5 6 7 8 9 10

GAME 2: 0 1 2 3 4 5 6 7 8 9 10 **GAME 4:** 0 1 2 3 4 5 6 7 8 9 10

22. Colours vocabulary flash cards

Unit 10, pages 190-191

Instructions

a. Before the class, print a set of flash cards to give each pair of students. Cut them out ready for the class. These cards could be used when you first clarify the vocabulary or the next day as revision.

b. Give the students the picture cards first without the words. They work in pairs to name the colours. Use the board to check the answers with the group. Go to www.esolbooks.com for free Power Point slides. You could consolidate this through shouting out a word/phrase for the students. They respond by holding up the picture and shouting out the number, e.g. Teacher: "blue!", students: "number 4!" If they find this easy, ask instead, "What's number 6?", students: "white!" Also, instruct the students to test each other in pairs, i.e. a student takes a card and asks their partner, "What's that?"

c. The students work in pairs to match the pictures to the words. Monitor to help, encouraging the learners to use the initial consonant and then check each group has done this correctly. This is enough in terms of checking answers as the gap-fill task on page 190 clarifies the spelling.

d. Use the board to show the words and elicit the initial consonant sounds and any interesting phonics, e.g. the silent letters in 'white.' Go to www.esolbooks.com for free Power Point slides.

e. The students remove the pictures so that they only have the words in front of them. Say the words (e.g. Teacher: "blue!") and the first student to hold up the word is awarded a point for their team. Finally, the students read the words on the cards aloud, in pairs.

f. If you used these cards to clarify the vocabulary, then the class can move to the initial consonant gap-fill on page 190.

1.	2.	3.
	4.	
5.	6.	7.
red	black	yellow
blue	orange	white
green		

23. Jobs vocabulary flash cards

Unit 12, pages 210-211

Instructions

a. Before the class, print a set of flash cards to give each pair of students. Cut them out ready for the class. These cards could be used when you first clarify the vocabulary or the next day as revision.
b. Give the students the picture cards first without the words. They work in pairs to name the words. Use the board to check the answers with the group. Go to www.esolbooks.com for free Power Point slides. You could consolidate this through shouting out a word/phrase for the students. They respond by holding up the picture and shouting out the number, e.g. Teacher: "cleaner!", students: "number 2!" If they find this easy, ask instead, "What's number 4?", students: "doctor!" Also, instruct the students to test each other in pairs, i.e. a student takes a card and asks their partner, "What's that?"
c. The students work in pairs to match the pictures to the words. Monitor to help, encouraging the learners to use the initial consonant and then check each group has done this correctly. This is enough in terms of checking answers as the gap-fill task on page 210 clarifies the spelling.
d. Use the board to show the words and elicit the initial consonant sounds and any interesting phonics, e.g. the 'er' in many of the jobs. Go to www.esolbooks.com for free Power Point slides.
e. The students remove the pictures so that they only have the words in front of them. Say the words (e.g. Teacher: "barber!") and the first student to hold up the word is awarded a point for their team. Finally, the students read the words on the cards aloud, in pairs.
f. If you used these cards to clarify the vocabulary, then the class can move to the initial consonant gap-fill on page 210.

1.

2.

3.

4.

5.

6.

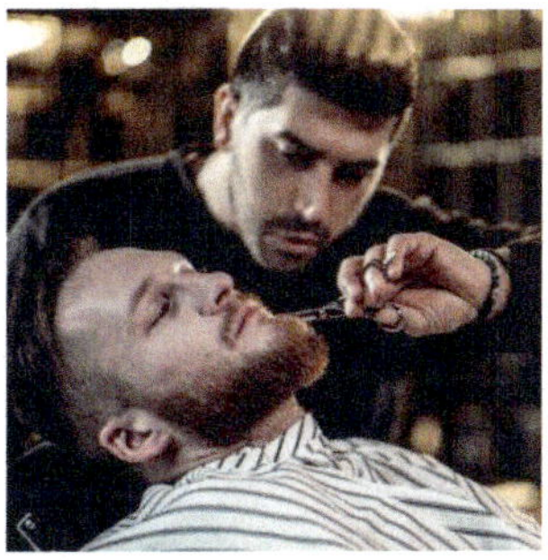

teacher	**cleaner**
barber	**doctor**
taxi driver	**farmer**

24. Signs flash cards

Unit 13, page 229

Instructions

a. Before the class, print a set of flash cards to give each pair of students. Cut them out ready for the class. Use these cards as revision the day after the work done using the Student's Book.
b. As a warm-up, ask the students to lay the cards out on their table. Describe a sign for the learners to pick up a card:

    1. It's 9 o'clock. I can go into the shop. It's NOT closed (open).
    2. Can I smoke cigarettes in college? No……? (No smoking)
    3. I have a cold and I need some tablets. Where can I go? (the pharmacy)
    4. It's 8 o'clock at night. The shop is NOT open. (closed)
    5. I need to go to the toilet (toilets).
    6. It's 4 o'clock and the class is finished. We can go home. Let's look for the …? (exit)

c. The students work in pairs to match two signs together, e.g. 'No smoking' as a picture with the one as text. Monitor to help and check the pairs have done this correctly.

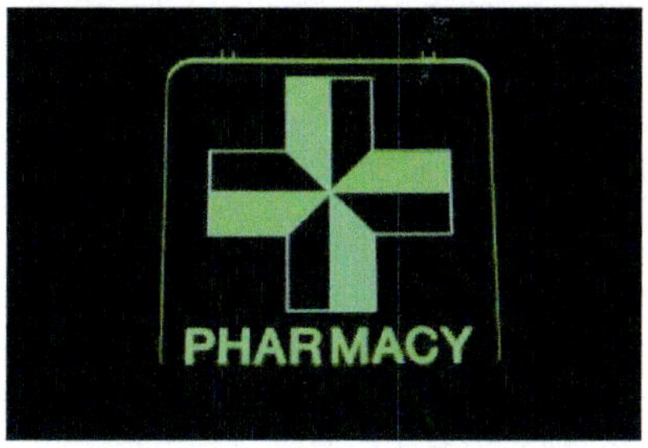
PHARMACY

NO SMOKING

TOILETS

EXIT

CLOSED

open

Closed

OPEN

25. Clothes vocabulary flash cards

Unit 14, pages 236-237

Instructions

a. Before the class, print a set of flash cards to give each pair of students. Cut them out ready for the class. These cards could be used when you first clarify the vocabulary or the next day as revision.

b. Give the students the picture cards first without the words. They work in pairs to name the words. Use the board to check the answers with the group. Go to www.esolbooks.com for free Power Point slides. You could consolidate this through shouting out a word/phrase for the students. They respond by holding up the picture and shouting out the number, e.g. Teacher: "jacket!", students: "number 2!" If they find this easy, ask instead, "What's number 5?", students: "t-shirt!" Also, instruct the students to test each other in pairs, i.e. a student takes a card and asks their partner, "What's that?"

c. The students work in pairs to match the pictures to the words. Monitor to help, encouraging the learners to use the initial consonant and then check each group has done this correctly. This is enough in terms of checking answers as the gap-fill task on page 236 clarifies the spelling.

d. Use the board to show the words and elicit the initial consonant sounds and any interesting phonics, e.g. the 'j' in 'jumper' and 'jacket' and its corresponding sound.

e. The students remove the pictures so that they only have the words in front of them. Say the words (e.g. Teacher: "hat!") and the first student to hold up the word is awarded a point for their team. Finally, the students read the words on the cards aloud, in pairs.

f. If you used these cards to clarify the vocabulary, then the class can move to the initial consonant gap-fill on page 236.

1. 	2. 	3. 
4. 	5. 	6. 
7. 	8. 	9. 
jeans	**jacket**	**shoes**
shirt	**t-shirt**	**hat**
dress	**jumper**	**glasses**

Games and warmers

We all know that students love games. These can be great to get the lesson off to a lively start or to lift the group if energy levels dip. Bear in mind the level of your class when you play these games, as some are appropriate for very basic level groups whereas more challenging activities would only be suitable for higher level ESOL Literacy learners.

1. **Stop the Bus!**

   This classic game involves learners working in pairs/small groups to think of one word beginning with a certain letter for several different categories. Model the task with a table like this written up on the board:

	Country	Food	Animal	I like....
S				

Elicit a word beginning with 's' for each category and board it. For example:

	Country	Food	Animal	I like....
S	Sudan	salad	snake	swimming

The first group to finish shouts, "Stop the bus!" although I now ask them to shout "Finished!" as they practise a more useful phrase. This game is not only fun but the learners also benefit from practising so many different language areas, e.g. vocabulary, initial consonants, spelling. For literacy learners, encourage them to try to write the words but students with very basic literacy skills can memorise some answers to give orally in open-class feedback instead of writing them down, if they struggle.

2. **What's in my bag?**

   This works best if you have a handbag or manbag, as I have. The students guess what's in your bag. For instance, they might shout out objects such as 'keys', 'phone', 'pen' etc. To add a competitive element, every time they get one correct you award them one point but the teacher gets a point if they get one wrong. The first to get, for instance, five points, is the winner!

3. **How many words?**
The teacher dictates phrases the students have recently learned and they have to count how many words you say. For example, if 'food' is your topic, a phrase could be, "I like chicken and rice." The students call out, "5 words!" Many thanks to my friend Karl Kaliski for suggesting this game to me.

4. **Dictation**
Dictate a word/phrase for the students to write down. You could use words that the students have learned recently or high-frequency Dolch/Fry's List words, e.g. have, go, do, like. The first student to call out the word is the winner. Dictating students' names is always quite good fun!

   A nice variation of this is the teacher 'writing' the word in the air with their finger. It's quite tricky though if you're facing your learners as you have to write backwards!

5. **Shout!**
Prepare slides or giant flash cards with words you've recently learned in class on them. The students need to read the word and shout it out. Put the students in teams and the first to shout out the word gets a point. Including your students' names is usually fun!

6. **Word tennis**
Separate the learners into small groups and choose a topic, for example, 'food.' Go round the groups in order and a student from each team needs to say a word from the topic. Set a time limit, e.g. 5 seconds, and clarify that they can't repeat a word that has already been used. Give them one chance with this rule, but after that teams are eliminated for repeating answers/running out of time. Last team standing gets a point. Other categories include drinks, animals, countries, clothes, hobbies, colours, jobs, sports/games, vehicles, everyday actions, things in your flat/kitchen/living room etc. Higher levels can manage more complex categories

such as technology, fruit, tools etc. This game is outlined in *English File* (Latham-Koenig C, Oxenden C and Lambert J [2018], Oxford: OUP).

7. **Kahoot**

   Kahoot involves students using their phones to answer quiz questions which the teacher prepares beforehand. You won't truly appreciate the frenzy that this can create until playing one in class with your students, especially if a game comes down to a tight finish. Quizzes which consolidate the work covered in *Read and Write every day* are available for free. You can find the Kahoots on www.esolbooks.com. Go to the extra materials section and navigate through to the relevant unit to find its Kahoot quiz. Alternatively, search ESOL_Books on Kahoot. You'll need to register an account.

8. **Guess the picture**

   Search for 'Guess the picture' on You Tube. You'll see an image but at first it's magnified and you just see a close-up, making it impossible. The image slowly zooms out and then the fun begins as students shout out their answers. This can be played with giant flashcards if technology is an issue: cover an A4 flashcard with a blank A4 card and gradually reveal the picture.

9. **Odd one out**

   This game is fun and really gets the class reading. Let's say the class have just learnt colours. Give them five words where four are colours but one isn't:

   red blue have green white

   They can do this in pairs and the first to finish is the winner. The complete version of this is on page 152. Alternatively, display the five words on the board for the students to shout out the answer. Another possibility is for students to find a word which is different according to spelling / phonics. For instance, 'chips' is different in the 5 words below as the others begin with 'sh.'

   shoe ship shop chips she

This can be effective as a review after a few months of the course as by then the class will have noticed a variety of sound-spelling combinations. Look at the example on page 153, for instance. If you create your own worksheet for this, try to use Fry's List / CVC words for the odd one out. It's a good idea to do these tasks orally before / instead of the worksheet, especially for weaker groups.

Colours

1.	red	blue	have	green	white
2.	black	yellow	green	get	red
3.	white	the	blue	black	pink
4.	red	blue	from	green	white
5.	brown	white	like	black	pink
6.	white	where	red	black	brown
7.	green	blue	red	green	read
8.	white	black	green	clock	blue
9.	red	blue	brown	bank	white
10.	red	blue	where	green	white

Which word is different?

1. to time taxi some today
2. big but be ball come
3. see meet moon feet tree
4. like time win fine five
5. day play today boy say
6. where when what was why
7. cleaning cooking sleeping read shopping
8. very reading every baby many
9. teacher paper barber chair river
10. at am on and all

10. Hit the board

Prepare a board with words you have learned recently or Dolch/Fry's list words. For example:

like
go
very
the from
my
for have
am to in

Two students come up to the board, you call out a word and they have to find it and touch it. The first to do so is the winner. Just do 3 and then change the pairs.

11. Running dictation

Some preparation is needed for this activity and bear in mind that it works best with smaller groups and an area that can be cleared easily. Write 6 or 7 short phrases on a piece of paper and stick this on the wall at the front of the class. Separate the students into small groups and assign some as 'scribes' and some as 'runners'. With basic ESOL Literacy groups, use phrases from a text you have read that week, in order to make this achievable and to consolidate language focused on during recent classes. For example:

1. I like chicken.
2. I don't like coffee.
3. I eat rice every day.
4. I drink tea every day.
5. I have dinner at 7:00.

The runners have to read a sentence, memorise it and then head to their scribe, sitting at the back of the room, to dictate it to them. The scribes have to write down the phrase, with some support with spelling from their runners and teacher. Go back and forth yourself to help the students and watch out for cheeky learners who take photos of the master sheet!

12. Flash cards

Flash cards are a great way to clarify vocabulary in a student-centred way. You will need to print and cut out the cards before class but they can be used over and over again. For instance, here are some flash cards from page 115 for students to learn a lexical set of vehicles.

bus	bike	boat
ship	train	taxi
van	plane	lorry

These are great for your group to learn vocabulary or can be used as revision the following day. In addition to this, there are some fun games the learners can play. With just the pictures laid out in front of them, the teacher can call out a word and the learners pick up the card and show it to the teacher. This can be repeated with a literacy aim by the students laying out just the words and the teacher once again saying the names of the vehicles. Literacy students can use the initial consonant sound to help them identify the word.

13. Pelmanism

A fun memory game which can be played using the flash cards in this book, like the ones above for vehicles. The students, working in pairs or small groups, separate the pictures and words. They then turn them all over so they are face down. They take it in turns to turn up one picture and one word, which they read aloud. The learners have to remember where the pictures and words are to collect matching sets.

14.I spy

The teacher thinks of an object in the room, for instance, 'cup' and tells the learners the first letter and sound. In the case of 'cup', the teacher says, "I can see something in the room which begins with letter 'c', sound /k/. What is it?" The students shout out their guesses, e.g. "Computer? Coke?

15.Kim's game

Another classic ESOL game in which the teacher prepares a document for the whiteboard of pictures representing words/phrases the students have learned recently. After the students name the pictures as revision, tell them that they have one minute to memorise all of them, after which you remove the images and they tell each other all the words. For example, here is the slide for the lexical set of vehicles:

Then show a prepared slide which is missing two of the pictures and where the remaining vehicles are mixed up:

The students shout out which pictures are missing. Visit www.esolbooks.com to access pre-prepared slides like these, for all the vocabulary areas focused on in *Read and Write every day*.

16.Colours

Throw a ball to a student and say a colour, e.g. "blue." The student names something which is blue, e.g. "The sky is blue." They throw the ball to another learner and choose a different colour, e.g. "yellow." The student says something which is yellow, e.g. "The sun is yellow." Colours can be used more than once but not objects. For example, the next time the colour blue is chosen, a student can't repeat 'sky' as their answer.

17.Banana Skin

You may know this game as 'hangman.' It's a good idea to avoid the traditional version of this involving a hangman's noose to protect students who have experienced trauma so here's a modern version. Draw a banana skin on the board and a stick man walking towards it. Choose a word/phrase the class have learned recently and board the corresponding number of lines, e.g. for the phrase, 'I go to college by bus', board this:

_ .

Nominate students to give you a letter and write in into the corresponding space(s), if they guess correctly. For instance, if they guess 'letter o' you board:

_ o _ _ o _ _ o _ _ _ _ _ _ _ _ _ _ _ _ _ _ _ _ .

If the letter is not in the word/phrase then the stick man goes a little closer to the banana skin. The game ends when the students identify the phrase or with the man's comedic slip on the banana skin!

18. Find a word

Write a mixture of vowels and consonants on the board, e.g.

p s l a t d e l m o u n

The learners, in pairs, write as many words as they can, using each letter just once, and look for the longest word, e.g. it, do, time.

19. Count up – count down

This game works well after learning numbers 1-10 or numbers up to 20. One student counts up while the other counts down. For example, student A: "1", student B: "10"; student A: "2", student B: "9"; student A: "3", student B: "8." It's possible with bigger numbers, e.g. numbers up to 100 can be practised if students count in tens, e.g. Student A: "10", student B: "100", student A: "20", student B: "90" etc.

20. Stand up if....

The teacher gives instructions and students stand up or stay seated accordingly. Examples of instructions:

Stand up if....

- you like college / homework / reading / writing / football etc
- you are a student / teacher / man / woman / barber / doctor
- you go to college on Monday / Tuesday / Saturday
- you go to college by bus / car / on foot / by helicopter
- you speak Arabic / Pashto / Kurdish
- you live in Glasgow / London / Paris
- you are from England / Iran / Sudan / Afghanistan
- you have a phone / an iPhone / a Samsung phone / a pencil / a bike / a car / a microwave / a garden
- you always bring a bag / book / pencil to college
- you had breakfast / a coffee / a cup of tea before college
- you have black / brown / blond hair/ a beard / a moustache / long hair / short hair
- you are wearing glasses / a black jacket / jeans / white shoes
- went swimming / shopping / to the gym yesterday
- you can drive / ride a horse / play the guitar / run fast /

Award a winner based on your own judgement of who stood up when it was correct to do so the most. If you can think of a points system then well done!

21. Simon says

The teacher gives an instruction but the students only act it out if it's preceded by "Simon says…." A variation could be "The teacher says…" or that the learners only carry out the action if the instruction finishes with, "please." Thanks to the You Tube channel, Mooncake English for this game.

22. Bingo

A great game to practise numbers. Give each pair a card and dictate various numbers until one of the groups crosses off all the numbers and shouts out "Bingo!" There are several games in the photocopiable materials section of this book. Here's an example of some cards from unit 11:

10	23	32
48	53	69
75	89	100

8	22	39
40	52	69
76	80	99

7	23	30
44	57	60
78	83	95

19	21	33
42	59	63
71	87	92

Bingo can also be played with words, for example, Dolch/Fry's List words or in the example below, with numbers in written form:

two	four
six	nine

one	five
six	ten

one	three
five	nine

two	five
six	ten

The following page is an example of Dolch List bingo:

go	have
to	and

am	my
the	get

my	go
from	to

like	have
to	get

like	am
have	to

live	my
go	and

go	my
from	the

am	live
the	to

like	and
from	have

Record of words called out:

GAME 1: my like have get to live from and am to the

GAME 1: my like have get to live from and am to the

GAME 3: my like have get to live from and am to the

23. I like TV

This game, which is also known as 'I went to the market', can be adapted depending on the current theme. Here's an example if your topic is 'free time.' The teacher starts by saying "I like TV." The next student has to repeat this and then add one more activity, e.g. "I like TV and shopping." Subsequent students repeat this but then add to it, for instance, "I like TV, shopping and the gym." This can be repeated for other topics/language areas. For example, if your topic is 'food', students could say "When I go shopping I always buy rice, chicken and juice." You can ramp it up in terms of language if appropriate, for instance, "I went shopping yesterday and I got....." Either go round the class student-by-student or take a ball to throw to decide whose turn is next and make it more random.

24. Student-teacher-read

The students work in two or three groups of about five students in each team during this game, which works particularly well if you have a large white board or even two boards/flipcharts. Alternatively, you could give each team a piece of A3 paper. The teams work independently with the teacher monitoring to help. The teacher boards a starting word, e.g. 'student' and one learner in each team writes a word beginning with the final letter of that word ('t'). For instance, they could write 'the', 'two' or 'teacher.' The student passes the pen to the next student to write a word beginning with the final letter of that word. So if the first learner writes 'the' then the next student could write 'every' and the subsequent group member, 'yes.' Encourage the students to collaborate over both the words to write next and the spelling. After a few minutes they should develop a list like this:

student

the

every

yes

Sudan

never

After 5 minutes, stop the game, award a point for each word written and the team with the most points is the winner.

25. Grapevine

Put the students into small groups, e.g. teams of six learners. Ideally, they sit in a line side-by-side. Give the first pair of students a list of words which they have learned recently, e.g.

1. do
2. the
3. have
4. go
5. like

The first pair has to read the first word and tell the pair sitting next to them along the line. The word is passed verbally along the line until it reaches the final pair, who write it down. Give other groups 5 different words. Alternatively, this could be done with phrases.

26. Word snakes

Board short phrases but with no spaces. The students have to work together to try to read them. For example:

1. IlikeTV.
2. Ilikeshopping.
3. IwatchTVeveryday.
4. Idon'tlikecooking.
5. Iamastudent.

A possible follow-up is that they copy the phrases but add spaces.

27. Noughts and crosses

Draw a noughts and crosses game on the board and populate it with letters, e.g.

c	d	f
g	h	t
n	f	s

Split the class into two teams, one team can be 'noughts' and one 'crosses' ('circles and crosses' might be an easier name for the game!). Team A chooses a letter and the teacher provides a definition/context to describe a word which begins with that letter. For instance, if they choose 'h' you could elicit 'holiday' by saying, "In the summer we don't go to college, some people go to a different city or country or just relax at home. I don't work, you don't go to college. What is this?" If they get it right they get a circle/cross, e.g.

c	m	f
g	h	t
n	c	s

The first team to get a line of three noughts/crosses wins.

28.Dolch/Fry's List bag

See page 12 for an explanation of the Dolch/Fry's List and the idea of students writing these onto separate cards. There are several games you can play with these in order to help the students consolidate their literacy skills and become familiar with the words. For example, they can lay the cards out on the table and pick up a card which the teacher calls out. They can then work in small groups, helping each other to read the words aloud. Finally, each student can take turns to pick a card from the pack and read it aloud without showing it to their classmates, who write it down in their notebooks. If any student is struggling, they can ask, "Show me" for a quick look!

29.Miming games

Miming games lend themselves well to certain topics. For example, if the students learn a lexical set for illness, then they can consolidate by working in a small group and taking turns to mime an illness for their classmates to guess. For example, they mime phrases such as "I have a cough", "I have a headache" etc. Emphasise to the class that they can't speak during this game.

I like to play a miming game on the last day of the term / year, using the cards on the following pages. Cut these cards out before class and then divide the class into two teams. Students take a card and mime for their classmates to guess. The student who shouts out the right word first wins a point for their team.

get up

drive a car

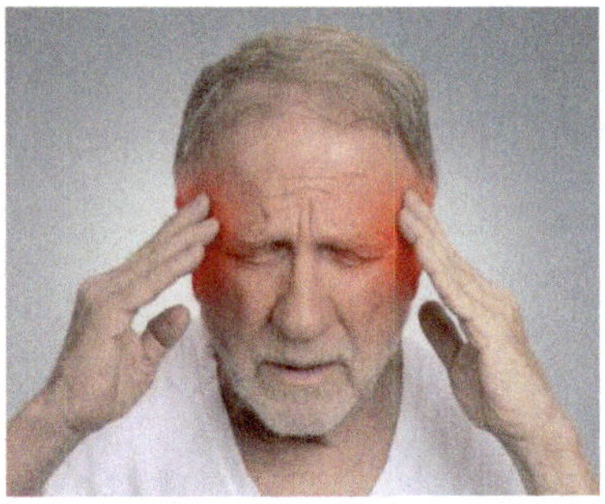

headache

fall down

happy

sad

 tired	 cold
 monkey	 horse
 scared	 angry

hungry

rubbish / bin

selfie

take a photo

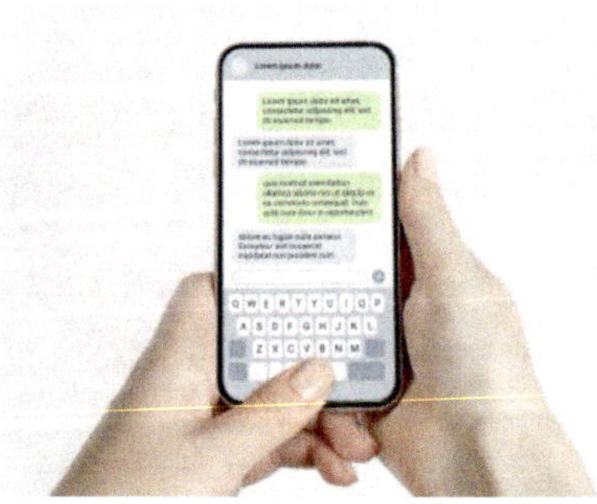

text my friend

noisy

watch TV

make a cake

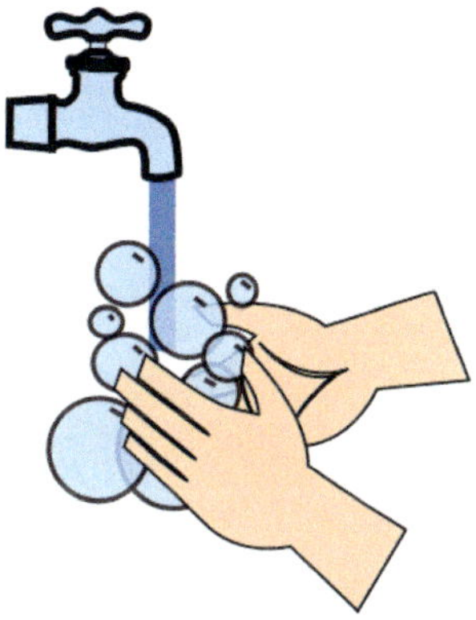

wash my hands

shopping

swimming

the gym

gaming

listen to music

chilli

banana

read a book

clean my flat

cut onions

bike

I'm eating ice cream

I'm eating spaghetti

I've lost my key.

dance

I'm making tea.

washing machine

play the guitar

play the piano

drums

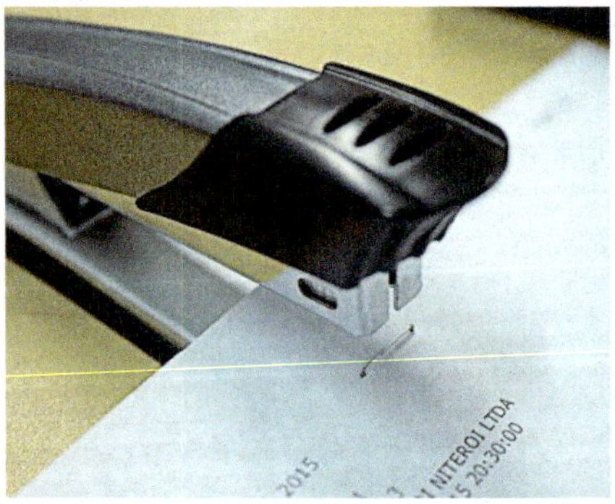

stapler

miss the bus

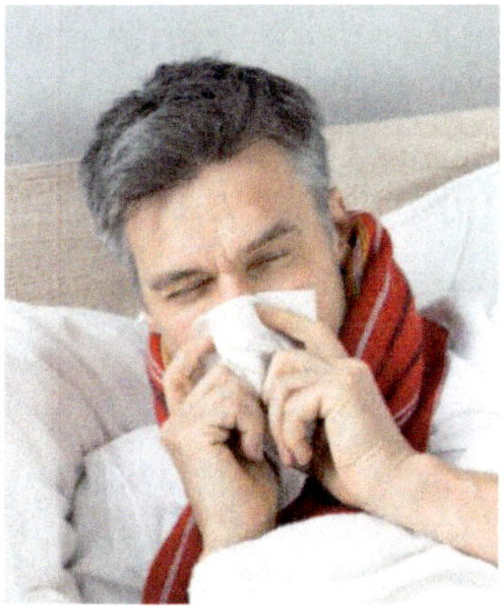

sick

painting

fishing

30. Pictionary

Another great game for the final day of the course. Students take a card and draw a picture for everyone to guess. Divide the students into teams to add a competitive element. Including yourself as one of the pictures to draw, if you're brave enough, usually leaves the class in stitches!

write

pencil

your teacher

cup of tea

cat

shopping

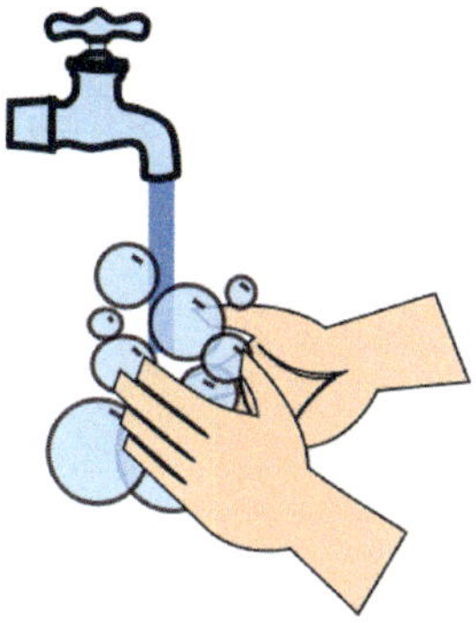

wash my hands

ship

watch

watch TV

shoes

fish

gaming

listen to music

swimming

the gym

football

sleep

reading

clean my flat

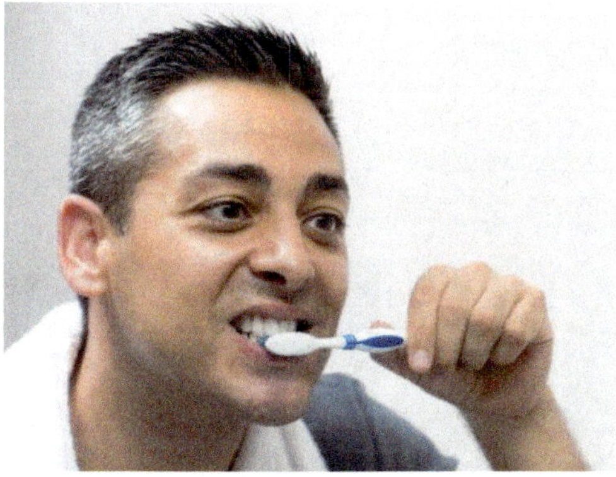

brush my teeth

shower

tree

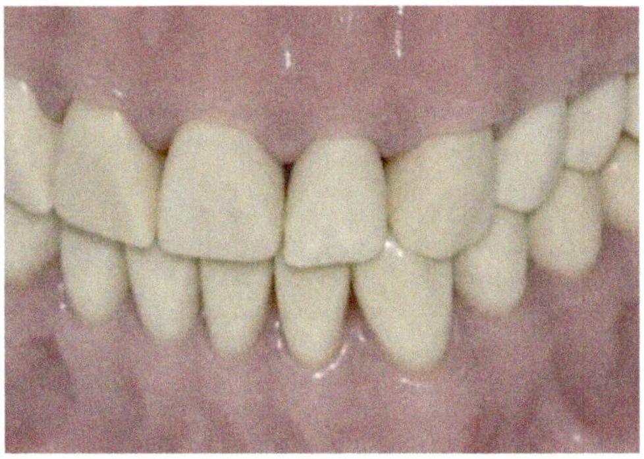

teeth

bike

bus

car

van

lorry

plane

train

helicopter

carrot

apple

tomato

keys

ice cream

eat

cooking

rice

onion

money

hot dog

chair

dog

raining

sofa

washing machine

No smoking

bin

barber

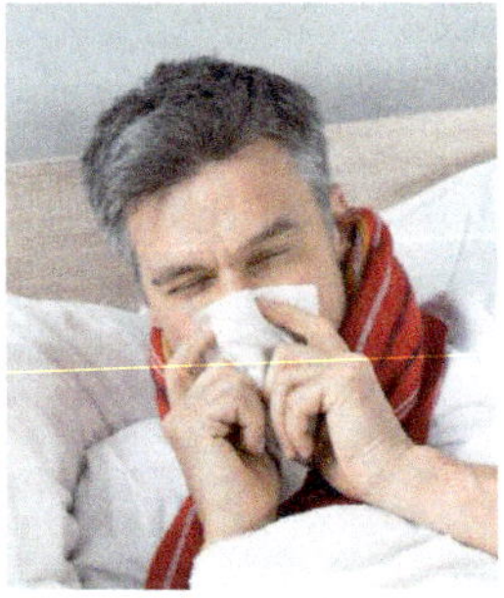

sick

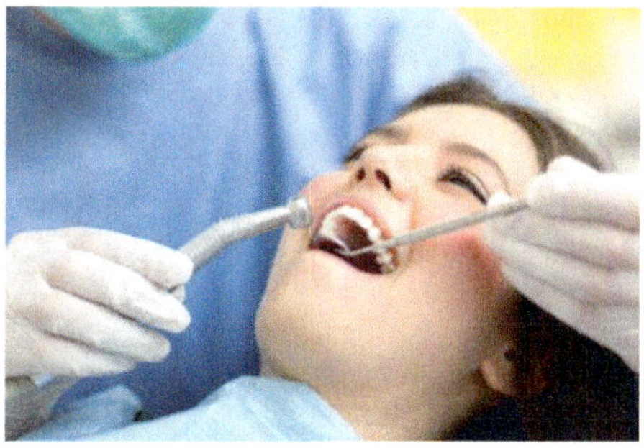

dentist

phone

glasses

beard

tiger

dress

t-shirt

hat

cake

dance

umbrella

sing

drums

fall down

guitar

piano

horse

pizza

mountain

house

rainbow

monkey

cow

bird

snake

spider

elephant

giraffe

crocodile

dolphin

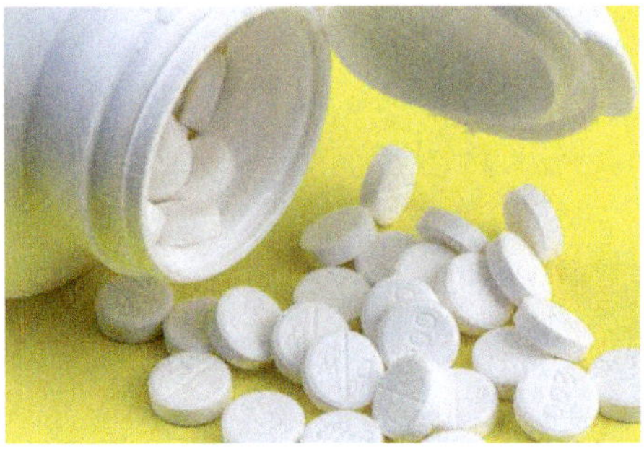 tablets	 the sea
 sharpener	 kettle
 sunglasses	 Father Christmas

firefighter

laptop

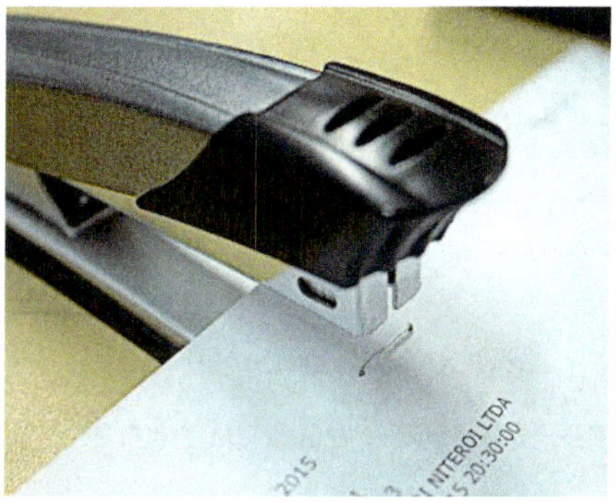

stapler

camel

exit

sheep

References

1. Burton, M (2007), 'Oral Reading Fluency for Adults', London: NRDC – Report focusing on the merits and challenges of reading aloud (available online at www.nrdc.org.uk).
2. Department for Education and Skills (2003), 'Skills for Life', Crown Copyright
3. English with Cambridge - You Tube channel.
4. Excellence Gateway - website with a range of online activities for ESOL students (search online for this as at time of publication a new site is under construction).
5. Latham-Koenig C, Oxenden C and Lambert J (2018), 'English File Beginner', Oxford: OUP
6. LLU+, 'Teaching Basic Literacy to ESOL Learners' DVDs, London: LLU+ (LLU+ no longer exists so this will be increasingly difficult to find unfortunately).
7. www.kahoot.com - website where you can create your own interactive quizzes to use in class.
8. www.manythings.org - website with interactive tasks for ESOL learners.
9. www.natecla.org.uk – National Association for Teaching English and Community Languages to Adults
10. SQA ESOL Literacies National 2 Learning Support Material (https://www.sqa.org.uk/sqa/33697.html)
11. Sunderland H and Spiegel M (2006), 'Teaching Basic Literacy to ESOL Learners', London: LLU+ - key book on the theory and practice of teaching ESOL literacy learners. Includes clarification of key concepts such as phonics, LEA, spiky profile etc, always with a practical eye on how to put these into practice in the classroom.
12. www.juicyenglish.com - features a list of different pronunciation drills which teachers can use to help students.
13. What's App - app for mobiles/desktop.
14. You Tube – videos app. Two games in the games section are from You Tube channels: Mooncake English and Guess the Picture.

Printed in Great Britain
by Amazon

56026636R00110